Updated Guide to Protecting Your Rights and Wallet

SELF-PUBLISHER'S LEGAL HANDBOOK

SECOND EDITION

HELEN SEDWICK

Author and Business Attorney

CONTENTS

CHAPTER ONE

INDIE AUTHORS TO THE RESCUE

THE SENSE OF community among self-publishing writers is inspiring.

On countless blogs and forums, we share tips about character development, formatting, and platform building. We cheer indie authors who win awards or nail spots on bestseller lists. We encourage one another when sluggish sales take their toll. I cannot think of any other business where so-called competitors share such a strong sense of purpose.

Indie authors are changing the publishing world. By some accounts, we earn 40% of all Kindle ebook revenues and account for 18% of sales in the overall book market. And we've only just begun.

Since I released the first edition of *Self-Publisher's Legal Handbook* in 2014, indie authors have taught me what legal questions worry them most. I've prepared an expanded edition of the *Handbook* to answer more questions. This second edition includes

- An expanded discussion about using real people in your writing,

- More details on how to deal with content theft and piracy,

- A chapter on when and how to adopt a pen name,

- More information about getting permission to use lyrics, images, and quotes,

- Additional nitty-gritty about the business side of writing, especially taxes,

- A discussion of estate planning for writers, and

- A look at opportunities beyond print and ebooks, including audio books and translations.

I am a business lawyer with 30 years of experience assisting clients in setting up and running their businesses, legally and successfully. My clients include entrepreneurs such as winery owners, green toy makers, software engineers, and writers. I do not go to court, and no one is ever going to produce a movie about the exciting life of a business attorney. But I get a great deal of satisfaction keeping my clients out of trouble so they can focus on their businesses, their creative projects, and their lives.

In addition to practicing law, I write fiction. Like most writers, I have my share of rejection letters, some personal and encouraging, and many cold and impersonal.

In 2012 I decided to self-publish my historical novel *Coyote Winds*. At first, the self-publishing process seemed daunting, impossible. Taking one step at a time, I discovered the process was not so difficult, thanks in no small part to all the information other writers shared in books and online. I love the sense of control over my work, something I would have lost taking the traditional publishing route.

I also discovered that many indie authors were struggling with legal questions ranging from how to protect their work to how to set up their businesses. The market was flooded with books giving them advice about designing covers, editing content, and tweeting effectively, but no one explained how to protect their Social Security Numbers or spot a scam.

I wrote *Self-Publisher's Legal Handbook* to help writers self-publish and promote their work while minimizing legal risks and errors.

- Chapter Two explains copyright basics every writer should know, including how to spot a "rights grab" and deal with content theft.

- Chapter Three looks at the legalities of using work created by others, including fair use and public domain.

- Chapter Four is an expanded discussion of using people in your writing, with real-life examples of cases involving defamation and invasion of privacy claims.

- Chapter Five explains when and how to use a pen name.

- Chapter Six provides an overview of the pathways for transforming a manuscript into a book, whether you hire a full-service self-publishing company or do it yourself.

- Chapter Seven demystifies the process of finding and hiring freelance editors, designers, and other professionals.

- Chapter Eight lays out the steps to setting up your self-publishing business.

- Chapter Nine looks at options for financing the production and marketing of your work.

- Chapter Ten is full of suggestions for writing a clever disclaimer.

- Chapter Eleven highlights key income tax and sales tax issues facing writers.

- Chapter Twelve discusses the legal issues of marketing and distribution, including buying reviews, sending mass emails, and selling books through bookstores.

- Chapter Thirteen identifies common scams and myths targeting writers.

- Chapter Fourteen covers estate planning for writers.

- Chapter Fifteen lists questions to ask before entering into a writing partnership.

- Chapter Sixteen explores opportunities beyond print and electronic books, including audio books, translations, and consulting.

You don't need to read the chapters sequentially. You could be working on transforming your manuscript into a paperback and ebook while you are setting up your business and designing your website. Copyright and defamation issues are ongoing, and taxes are forever. I reference useful websites throughout the book, and you will find web addresses for them at the end of the *Handbook* under Resources and on my website (http://helensedwick.com).

Like most business attorneys, I blend legal and business advice. The most cautious legal advice is useless if it makes no business sense. But an aggressive business strategy that crosses over the legal line is just as useless and potentially more damaging. Even if you are writing a book about how to rob a bank or hack the Pentagon, readers expect you to deal with them honestly and competently. Lose a reader's trust, and you'll lose that reader.

A few disclaimers:

- Although I am a lawyer, I am not *your* lawyer. Reading this book does not create an attorney-client relationship between us.

- This *Handbook* provides general legal information only, not legal advice. When a lawyer applies the law to your particular situation, that's legal advice.

- If you ask an attorney a question, her favorite answer will be "it depends." Legal outcomes depend on the particular facts and personalities involved. The information in this book is general in nature and may not apply to your specific situation.

- I am not soliciting you to send me legal work. Frankly, my plate and practice are already quite full.

- I am licensed to practice in the State of California only. While much of what I say applies in other states, I do not know the law in all 50 states, much less foreign jurisdictions.

- I provide links and references to other resources as a convenience to you. My links and references are not meant to imply an approval, endorsement, affiliation, sponsorship, or any other relationship to the linked resource or its operator.

- I will not tell you, *"Don't worry about it. No one will ever know."* I will lay out the law and customary practices. I may suggest a path intended to avoid legal landmines. Whether you follow the law is up to you. Some people enjoy the thrill of living near the edge; others have trouble sleeping when they take any risk.

- If you ask, *"Should I put it in writing?"* the answer is *yes*. Often the process of putting an agreement into writing reveals potential problems long before they turn into messy conflicts.

- And finally, the IRS requires that I say the following: *CIRCULAR 230 DISCLAIMER: If and to the extent that this material contains any tax advice, I am required by the Internal Revenue Service's Circular 230 (31 CFR Part 10) to advise you that such tax advice is not a formal legal opinion and was not intended or written to be used by you, and may not be used by you, (i) for the purpose of avoiding tax penalties that might be imposed on you or (ii) for promoting, marketing or recommending to another party any transaction or matter addressed herein.* In plain language, if you get in trouble with the IRS, you won't be able to avoid a penalty by saying that Helen Sedwick told you so. Sorry, folks. Compared to the IRS, I am powerless.

Let's read on.

CHAPTER TWO

COPYRIGHT BASICS

DID YOU KNOW that Andy Weir's *The Martian* started as a self-published ebook?

When sales took off, the audio book publisher Podium Publishing sought him out to produce an audio book that went on to win awards. Weir was then approached by an agent, and together they sold the publishing rights to a major publisher and the film rights to 20th Century Fox for mega-bucks.

You could be next.

Your writings are potentially valuable property and are entitled to protection, just like your car and your home. Let's take a look at what you own and how to protect it.

What Every Writer Should Know

Your interest in your manuscript is called a *copyright interest*. Copyright is a form of intellectual property, which means it's a product of the mind instead of the hand. Like most property, your copyright interest may be sold, assigned, licensed, given away, and bequeathed to your heirs.

As the copyright holder, you have the exclusive right to do the following:

- Reproduce the work in books or other formats,
- Sell, distribute, and commercially exploit the work,

- Create derivative works, such as translations, adaptations, sequels, abridgements, films, plays, apps, and

- Display or perform the work publicly, either live or in recorded form.

You make money from your work by granting others permission to publish, record, dramatize, translate, or otherwise commercially exploit your work in exchange for royalties or other compensation.

If anyone violates those exclusive rights, you have a claim of *infringement* against the wrongdoer. Of course, there are exceptions. The most common is *fair use*, which I'll discuss later in this chapter.

Copyright protects ownership of the *contents* of a writing or the image of a painting, not the physical letter, book, or painting itself. Someone who buys a copy of your book does not have the right to reprint, translate, or create a film from your book. He or she does have the right to read the copy, give it away, lend it to others, resell it, or toss it.

Similarly, if you have a love letter sent to you years ago, you own the physical letter, but that does not mean you may publish the contents of that letter because the copyright is held by the writer of the letter. Or, if you own the original of a painting, you do not have the right to use an image of that painting on your book cover. Merely owning a physical representation does not transfer ownership of the underlying intellectual property. Those are separate rights.

Copyright Attaches Automatically.

You own the copyright in your work as soon as you put an original creation into a fixed form, whether on a pad of paper, a hard drive, a smartphone, or a recording device. Your first draft, riddled with typos, inconsistencies, and clichés, is protected by copyright law whether or not you polish it, publish it, register it, or mark it with a ©.

Many people still assume you must publish, mark, and register your copyright for it to remain valid. That used to be the case until 1977. Since then, copyright ownership attaches easily and automatically.

Original does not mean Pulitzer Prize material. It means the work was not copied and contains some original expression. For instance, the listing of names and phone numbers in a phone book is not protected by copyright.

What's Protected by Copyright Law?

The most obvious categories cover literary works, musical works including lyrics, dramatic works, graphic and sculptural works, sound recordings, architectural works, and pantomimes and choreographic works if fixed in tangible form such as a video recording.

What about characters and settings? Maybe. If a character is as fully developed as Harry Potter or a setting as distinctive as Panem in *The Hunger Games*, the creator might claim copyright protection.

What's Not Protected by Copyright Law?

It varies from country to country.

In the United States, titles, names, and short phrases are copyright free. Sorry to say, your book's title is not protected by copyright in the United States. That's why there are so many books with similar titles.

If you have a series of books with a distinctive name, such as the *For Dummies* series, or a famous title such as *The Da Vinci Code*, you may have a *trademark* interest in the title, but only because that title has become associated in the minds of buyers with a particular book from a particular maker. Trademark rights are not automatic. A trademark arises when it is used and known in the marketplace, unlike copyright, which attaches automatically. I cover trademarks later in this chapter.

Objective information, such as historical facts, test results, and statistics, is not protected by copyright law, although the method of organization and analysis may be.

Real-world events are not protected. The estate of John Steinbeck does not own exclusive rights to write about the Dust Bowl. Anyone else may write about those same events.

Works that are not fixed into a tangible form of expression, such as improvisational performances and choreographic works that have not been written or recorded, are copyright free.

Ideas, themes, plot lines, and concepts, such as a spicy romance between space aliens, are not protected by copyright. This drives some writers crazy. They are sure their book ideas are worth millions and someone will steal them. Sorry. What copyright protects is the execution and expression of the idea into a story, drama, movie, painting, or piece of music—not the idea itself.

Stock characters and stereotypes, such as the tough-talking gangster or the handsome-but-dull hero, are not protected because they are not considered original. Same with generic settings such as deep space or undersea worlds.

Copyright Notice Is Not Required.

Marking your work with a © is no longer required for your rights to remain valid, but you should mark your work anyway. If your work is properly marked, then an infringer may not claim to be an "innocent infringer," and you may recover a larger award. The copyright notice has three parts:

1. © or copyright.

2. Year of first publication, which means the year the work was first distributed to the public. On unpublished material, the notice reads "Unpublished Work © year author."

3. Name of copyright owner, which may be a pen name or the name of an entity, such as a corporation. If there is more than one copyright owner, all of them should be named.

Also add "All Rights Reserved" because the phrase is required in some foreign countries. In Europe another common phrase is, "The moral rights of the author have been asserted."

Copyright Last a Long Time.

A copyright created in the United States today lasts for the life of the author plus 70 years. If there are two or more authors, it lasts for the life of the last surviving author plus 70 years. The copyright passes to the heirs of the owners like any other property interest. If the author is a corporation or other entity, then the copyright lasts 95 years from first publication, but not longer than 120 years after creation of the copyrighted material.

If the copyright was created in the United States before 1977, then the copyright may have expired, depending on whether the work was properly marked with a copyright notice, when and whether the work was registered, and whether the registration was renewed.

Registration Is No Longer Required.

Many people say they "copyrighted" their work when they mean they *registered* the copyright with the United States Copyright Office. You own the copyright in your work as soon as you put it into tangible form. Registering the copyright is an optional additional step and a good idea. Registration establishes a public, searchable record of your claim and is required before an infringement suit may be filed. Prompt registration (within three months following publication) increases the damages recoverable in an infringement action. Even if you miss that three-month window, you may—and should—still register the copyright in your book.

Undoubtedly, you will hear about "poor man's copyright" where you send yourself a copy of your own manuscript and keep the unopened, postmarked envelope as proof of what your manuscript looked like on that date. Don't bother. A poor man's copyright has no legal significance. Postmarks are too easy to fake. You are better off registering your work properly.

You can register your work online with the U.S. Copyright Office for $35; then you send in two copies of your work. I have had books lost by the Copyright Office, so I recommend sending them *certified mail, return receipt requested.*

You can also register website and blog content. I wrote a long post about the process, so check out my blog for more information.

The registration process may take up to a year, and your application may be listed as "incomplete" for months. Don't worry about the delay. The effective date of registration will be the date you submitted your application, not the date the copyright certificate is issued months later.

You may publish your book while you are waiting for your registration certificate without diminishing or affecting your copyright interest.

Copyrights Are Recognized Internationally.

Although there is no such thing as an international copyright, most developed countries have signed treaties that provide reciprocal recognition of copyrights. But no law makes a manuscript bulletproof against infringement. If your book is at all successful, then it will be pirated. If the infringers are overseas, there is little you can do without spending an inordinate amount of time and money. I discuss your options later in this chapter.

Copyrights Are Transferrable.

Even though writers say they "sell" their work, they are rarely transferring ownership. What they are selling are *licenses*. A license is a *right or permission to use* only; you, the creator, retain ownership of the copyrighted work. (In contrast, an *assignment* transfers complete ownership. It is rarely appropriate in publishing or self-publishing, except in a freelance or ghostwriting project if you understand up-front you are transferring all your rights and ownership in the work.)

Licenses may be exclusive or nonexclusive; worldwide or geographically restricted; short-term or perpetual; royalty free or royalty paying; or limited to particular media such as audio books, print, ebooks, or a particular language. The permutations are endless.

A license is similar to a lease. Imagine you are a landlord of a shopping center, and you lease shops to various tenants. Each lease is like an exclusive license granted to only one user. Other licenses, such as the right to use the parking lot, are non-exclusive, meaning more than one tenant may use them.

Your goal is to lease/license to each shopkeeper/licensee only the space it can actually use. If a shop/licensee sells ebooks in English only, you do not want to grant them the right to produce audio books in Spanish, etc. You don't want to tie up rights with someone who cannot use them to generate royalties for you.

Licenses

How are you going to know whether you are granting licenses that are too broad? You are going to have to read the contract.

To many people, contracts look like 5,000 words run through a blender. To simplify the reading, don't start at the beginning of the contract. Go straight to the section that deals with the granting of rights, typically titled License, Ownership, or Permissions. If that section is unacceptable (I'll explain what to look for), then you don't need to wade through the rest.

In *traditional publishing,* where the publisher is investing its own money in editorial, design, and marketing, a writer should expect to grant exclusive rights to the publisher. Even then, the writer should try to limit the license to the market the publisher actually serves. The relationship between author and publisher should be synergistic; both should benefit. If a publisher can't help you reach a particular market, then you should be reluctant to grant the publisher exclusive rights to that market.

Yet many traditional publishers, even small ones, ask for the world. Here is an example of an over-reaching contract from a small publisher of print and ebooks:

> *Author grants Publisher an exclusive, transferable, perpetual, worldwide license to print, publish, and sell in book, ebook, audio book, or in any form or format, in whole or in part, now known or hereafter invented in any language throughout the world during the life of the copyright, the Work as well as any derivative work including film, video, television, stage, and other dramatizations, created now or in the future.*

Translation: the author is granting the publisher virtually all rights to the book in all formats (including film rights) in all languages, for the life of the author plus 70 years! This is a rights grab and much too broad. I would not want to grant to this small book publisher the right to publish audio books, future formats, translations, films, or other derivative works. The publisher does not have the capacity to market in those areas. To return to the shopping center analogy, I would want to keep the lease/license as small as I could negotiate.

Here is an example of a narrower and more appropriate license for a traditional publishing deal:

> *Author hereby grants to Publisher the sole and exclusive right to publish (i.e., print, publish, and sell) the Work in print and digital (ebook) formats, in the English language, in the United States of America, its territories and dependencies, and in Canada, during the term of this Agreement and any renewals and extensions thereof, except as provided herein.*

See the difference? Narrow, specific, limited, lovely.

Almost every contract is negotiable. If the other side tells you the contract is standard and everyone signs it, don't believe them. Negotiate.

In *self-publishing*, licenses and grants of rights are almost always non-exclusive. That way you may sell print books through CreateSpace, IngramSpark/Lightning Source, and your own website, and sell ebooks via Amazon, Smashwords, iBooks, and other vendors, all at the same time.

There are exceptions, such as KDP Select, where writers agree to sell their ebooks exclusively through Amazon for a 90-day period. However, that's a short-term marketing program, not a long-term commitment.

Here's an example of a writer-friendly grant of rights in the self-publishing context:

> *Author grants Outskirts Press a NON-EXCLUSIVE, worldwide license to distribute and sell the manuscript in print and/or digital form; author grants Outskirts Press the non-exclusive right to exhibit manuscript in part on websites or promotional materials owned by Outskirts Press. Author grants Outskirts Press the non-exclusive right to store and transmit digital versions of manuscript to facilitate production, distribution, and sale of manuscript.*

This provision is limited to print and digital and is non-exclusive. Perfect.

Avoid any contract that has a *granting clause* that looks like this provision from an Author Solutions contract:

> *Throughout the Term of this Agreement, You grant to Us the exclusive, transferable, worldwide license to manufacture, store, use, display, execute, reproduce (in whole or in part), transmit, modify (including to create derivative works), import, make, have made, offer to sell, print, publish, market, distribute, and sell (individually or as part of compilations of collective works), and license for use via any subscription model, through all distribution channels (now or hereafter known, including online and electronic distribution channels), and otherwise exploit in any language, in print form, digital format, audio-book format, or via any other medium, now known or hereafter devised, the Work.*

Translation: they have total control over the distribution and development of the work until you terminate the contract.

Book Titles

Anyone who has written a novel will tell you how difficult it is to come up with a title that is resonant and eye-catching, so it is ironic that titles are not protected: they are considered too short to contain sufficient "original expression."

But there may be a way to protect your book title: trademark law. But not all titles will qualify as trademarks; your title must satisfy the criteria outlined below.

- *The title must be unique and distinctive.* Go to Amazon and search "betrayed." You'll find more than 25 books with that title. If your title consists solely of one or more common words, then you can write off claiming it as a trademark with one exception that I'll discuss below. For trademark purposes, the best titles are unique, made-up words like *Swamplandia* or *Freakonomics*.

- *The title must be more than merely descriptive.* Purely descriptive titles, such as *Hiking Trails of the Sierras* or *How to Trim an Apple Tree*, are rarely trademarks. The same rule applies even if the descriptive title is abstract or spiritual. I doubt you could claim a trademark in titles such as *Releasing Your Inner Yogi* or *Surviving Divorce*. Again, those titles are descriptive.

- *The title has become well known.* If you have a common or a descriptive title, all is not lost. If your book is so successful that consumers associate the title primarily with your book, then the title has achieved "secondary meaning" and might be considered a common law trademark. The *Twilight* series is a perfect example.

- *Your book is part of a series.* You are more likely to gain trademark status for the name of a series of books, such as *Harry Potter, Diary of a Wimpy Kid*, and the *For Dummies* line.

- *The title is part of a broader business venture.* If your book grew out of (or grows into) a larger enterprise such as consulting, public speaking, workshops, podcasts, or merchandising, then your title and related phrases are trademarks (for example, *Freakonomics*).

Trademark protection is not automatic. If you want to explore whether trademark protection and registration make sense for your titles, consult with a trademark attorney.

Content Theft

Sooner or later, every blogger and author suffers that dreadful moment of finding his or her work stolen. Either websites are offering free downloads of the books or blog scrapers are reposting material without permission or attribution.

Content theft is big business. Every month Google receives more than 30 million requests to remove search results that link to allegedly infringing material. Thirty million a month!

The good news is that writers have options for dealing with content theft, and 99% of the time they will not need an attorney. A little research and a few emails may do the trick.

First, to discourage unauthorized reposting of your online material:

- *Put a Copyright Notice in the footer of each web page.* The form is "*Copyright* or © + *date(s)* + *name of the copyright owner. ALL RIGHTS RESERVED.*"

- *Adopt a Copyright Policy.* Spell out the rules for people who want to quote your blog. A typical policy says something like this: *You may copy up to 50 words without permission provided you give attribution, link back to the original content, and do not change the overall meaning or message.* Put a link to your policy at the bottom of each web page.

- *Link back to your own blog.* Put links in your posts that direct people to other blog posts or other pages on your website. Your analytics software should notify you of "ping backs" so you can see who is displaying the link.

- *Register the copyright in your web content.* Many people don't realize that you can register the copyright on your blog and website material. There are a few tricks that I cover on my blog in the post "How to Register Your Blog with the U.S. Copyright Office."

- *Set up Google Alerts.* Not only for your name, but for your headlines and perhaps a string of unique words in your posts.

- *Investigate technology tools.* Various tools help bloggers disable right-clicks, watermark their work, or imbed devices for alerting them of repostings. For instance, Blasty.com is beta testing a new service that will monitor Google for unauthorized uses of your content, send you alerts, and allow you to send a takedown notice with one click or "blast." Considering the interest in fighting piracy, I expect this service and others should be quite successful.

Sooner or later, you will find sites offering free downloads of your books or reposting your web content. Then take the following steps:

- *Contact the site directly.* Believe it or not, some people still think everything on the internet is free to use. In most cases, if you email the infringing site, they will remove your material. You may even get an apology.

- *Send a takedown notice.* If an email request does not work, or you are dealing with a site that is offering free downloads, send a takedown notice under the Digital Millennium Copyright Act (DMCA).

All writers should learn how to send takedown notices. Like locking your car or home, it's easy and sensible. Social media sites such as YouTube, Tumblr, Pinterest, and Facebook have online forms for sending takedown notices. Typically, you'll find them under links titled Legal, Copyright, Report a Problem, or Help.

If you are dealing with an infringing website, you should send the takedown notice to the ISP hosting the infringing site. Go to http://whois.net/ and type in the domain. Many ISPs have online forms for sending takedown notices. If there is no online form, the website Plagiarism Today has downloadable samples of a cease-and-desist letter and DMCA takedown notice.

- *Notify search engines.* Use the Google Copyright Infringement Reporting Tool to request that the infringing site be removed from their search results. Contacting Google is important. You don't want the bogus sites to appear above legitimate ones in search results.

Once the social media site, ISP, or search engine receives a takedown notice, it contacts the alleged infringer. If the infringer does nothing, then the infringing material is taken down. End of story.

If the infringer disputes your claim, they may file a DMCA counter notification. In that case, the online service will repost the infringing material unless you notify them within 14 business days that you have filed a legal action against the alleged infringer. If the ISP is not based in the United States, it may simply ignore the takedown notice. In either of these cases, skip to Hiring an Attorney.

Piracy and Knock-Offs

Some thefts don't stop at copying blog posts; they steal entire books or create knock-offs with confusingly similar titles. Amazon has an ongoing problem with ebooks intended to trick buyers into purchasing the wrong product. Both *Thirty-Five Shades of Grey* and *I Am the Girl with the Dragon Tattoo* (both fakes) sold thousands of copies before they were removed from Amazon's site. Here are some options for ebook authors:

- *Set up Google Alerts*, as I discussed earlier.

- *Contact Amazon and other retailers.* If you find an infringing book, Amazon will work with you to remove infringing materials or confusing knock-offs. Their copyright claims procedures can be found at Notice and Procedure for Making Claims of Copyright Infringement. For other sites, contact them through their website.

- *Register your copyright.* If you have not already done so, register the copyright for the work. You cannot file a lawsuit unless the work is registered with the U.S. Copyright Office. If you threaten to sue, and the infringer searches copyright records and doesn't find your registration, they may call your bluff.

Hiring an Attorney

If the infringement continues despite your efforts, then consider hiring an attorney. A cease-and-desist letter on lawyer letterhead may be taken more seriously.

However, I would not hire an attorney or jump into litigation without asking yourself whether it will be worth the effort. Sure, if you sue and win, you may be entitled to collect damages, but your damages (lost sales) may be small and difficult to prove. The infringer may be overseas and unreachable. And litigation consumes money like wildfire, not to mentioned time, attention, and sleep.

Before you accuse someone of infringement or send a DMCA takedown notice, keep the following in mind:

- Titles are not copyrightable. If someone uses a title similar to yours, you cannot claim copyright infringement. Sorry.

- Ideas, themes, facts, and historical events are not protected by copyright. If someone publishes work covering topics similar to yours, that is not automatically infringement. Infringement implies close copying of how you expressed ideas and information, not the actual ideas and information themselves.

- If someone is quoting your work for commentary, educational, or review purposes, or creating a parody of your work, that is probably fair use and *not* infringement, no matter how scathing.

- Those sites offering cheap or free PDFs of your book are typically scams that download malware and harvest email addresses and credit card numbers. Anyone who clicks on those sites is unlikely to buy your book anyway.

- Don't get caught up in a game of whack-a-mole. While it's upsetting to see your work stolen or used as bait, the theft may have little economic consequence to you. You could waste a lot of time chasing these lowlifes. As soon as you deal with one, others will pop up. Your energy may be better spent creating new work and finding new readers.

Protecting Ideas

Many writers are distressed to hear that ideas are not protected by copyright. After all, aren't ideas the core of creative work and the spark most worth protecting?

Think about it. How many times have you had what seemed like a brilliant idea, but when you sat down to turn it into a book, the idea sputtered out around page 30, or page 5, or page 2? An idea has little value unless you craft it into something more. It's the execution of the idea that is valuable and protectable.

However, if you want to enhance the protection of your ideas and manuscript, ask freelancers, agents, editors, and beta readers to sign a non-disclosure agreement (NDA). I have posted a sample NDA on my blog (http://helensedwick.com/can-your-million-dollar-idea-be-protected/).

For freelancers and beta readers, asking for an NDA is reasonable. However, if you are talking about your project on your blog or a writer's forum, you can't expect your freelancer or reader to be bound to keep confidential what you have already made public.

Most agents and publishers will flat out refuse to sign an NDA. I doubt they are planning to steal your ideas, but they may already be working on something similar and fear you will accuse them of stealing. In fact, many agents and publishers will require you to sign a submission release that looks something like this:

> *Agent and/or any of its clients may have created, may create, or may otherwise have access to materials, ideas, and creative works which may be similar or identical to your material with regard to theme, motif, plots, characters, formats, or other attributes; and you shall not be entitled to any compensation because of the proposed use or use of any such similar or identical material.*

> *You agree that you will not assert against Agent or any of its clients any claim based upon infringement, plagiarism, breach of confidentiality, breach of implied contract,*

unfair competition, theft of ideas, concepts or characters, or any other claim arising
out of the use or alleged use of my manuscript.

Submissions are common in the film industry, but are still rare in the book world. If you don't want to sign one, don't submit your work to the agents and publishers who require them.

DRM

DRM, short for *digital rights management,* stands for any software or hardware device that deters unauthorized copying or viewing of content such as ebooks, music, and film. It is the lock and key for digital copyrighted material. Any digital file downloaded without DRM is easily copied.

If you publish your ebook through Kindle Direct Publishing (KDP), then you have the option of adding DRM to your work. But Smashwords and other ebook publishers and distributors will not accept ebooks with DRM. Surprised? I was.

DRM is controversial. You wouldn't think so. You work months or years on a book. Of course, you put a lock on it to protect it against unauthorized copying and piracy. You lock your home and your car—why not your *intellectual property?*

Mark Coker, founder of Smashwords, explained his reasons for discouraging DRM:

- Printed books never die. They are lent to friends, donated to libraries, and sold as used books, and no one calls that piracy. Why impose tighter restrictions on ebooks?

- "Obscurity is a bigger threat to authors than piracy." I heard Mark say these words at a conference, and despite my dreams of being a *New York Times* bestselling author, I have to admit he is correct. I have given away hundreds of books intentionally, so maybe a few more are being given away unintentionally. The more people read my book, the more likely word-of-mouth will spread. And let's face it, word-of-mouth sells books.

- The vast majority of readers are willing to pay a fair price for a good read. True, so far. I wonder how long that will last as we grow more accustomed to obtaining reading material on the internet for free.

- DRM doesn't work. Remember when the music industry tried to control unauthorized downloads by adding DRM? Remember people getting arrested? Well, that blew up in the face of the music industry as more people began to download music illegally out of spite, and software geeks proved getting around DRM was a piece of cake. DRM doesn't stop the crooks. Of course, people say the same about locking one's house, but I still do it.

By the way, you do not need DRM to protect your copyright. Some people worry that not applying DRM to their intellectual property is equivalent to donating their work to the public domain. Legally speaking, no. You still own the copyright. But I recommend authors put a copyright notice and "All Rights Reserved" near the front of their ebooks to put the world on notice of ownership.

Protecting Your Rights Checklist

After reading this chapter, you have a better understanding of the bundle of rights known as copyright, including

- ☐ how a copyright is created, licensed, and protected,
- ☐ what is covered by copyright and what is not,
- ☐ why it's important to register your copyright,
- ☐ how to spot an overreaching license,
- ☐ which titles may be protected by trademark,
- ☐ how to deal with content theft,
- ☐ when to ask for a non-disclosure agreement, and
- ☐ the pros and cons of DRM.

Now let's look at how to use work created by others.

CHAPTER THREE

USING WORK CREATED BY OTHERS

ABOUT ONCE A week, I get an email that reads something like this: "*I found the perfect image for my book cover on the internet. I may use it legally, can't I, as long as I give credit to the photographer?*"

Legally speaking, no.

Many people make the mistake of thinking that simply giving credit to the original illustrator, photographer, or writer is enough to protect them from a claim of copyright infringement. It's not.

Any time you use a work created by someone else, whether it's an image, a quote, or a few lines of lyrics, you need to consider two things:

- Is the work covered by copyright?
- Will your use infringe on that copyright?

Not all creative works are subject to copyright, and not all uses are infringement. How are you to know? Here are some guidelines.

Is the Work Subject to Copyright?

There are four major categories of works that are not protected by copyright and are therefore in the *public domain*. Any work in the public domain is free to use without permission or compensation. You should, however, always give credit to the original creator out of respect and to avoid plagiarism. Plagiarism is not a legal claim; it's an ethical standard.

1. The copyright has expired.

The most common reason a copyrighted work falls into the public domain is the copyright has expired. For example, Shakespeare's plays, Mozart's sonatas, and Leonardo da Vinci's *Mona Lisa* are all in the public domain.

The following works created in the United States are in the public domain because the copyright has expired:

- Any work first published before 1923

- Any unpublished work created before 1895

- Any unpublished work created by someone who died before 1945

For works published between 1923 and 1977, the expiration depends on whether a copyright notice was properly placed, whether the copyright was registered, and whether the registration was renewed. For works published after 1977, the copyright won't expire until 70 years after the author's death. The duration of copyrights for works created in different countries may be different.

For example, suppose you want to use the lyrics of *Take Me Out to the Ballgame* in your novel. With a little internet research, you'll find that the lyrics were first published in 1908. Its copyright has expired, and you would not be infringing on the songwriters' copyright by using the lyrics.

Keep in mind that only the sheet music and lyrics as they were published in 1908 are in the public domain. Lyrics or arrangements added after 1922 may still be protected by copyright.

Many museums and libraries provide downloadable images of public domain works, such as Renaissance paintings and Greek sculptures. Don't be surprised if they charge a small "reproduction" fee for the right to download a high-resolution image. They are trying to cover the costs of maintaining the website. Some sites will say you may download and use their images for non-commercial use only. Frankly, I doubt that's an enforceable restriction.

2. The work was created by the U.S. federal government.

If an image was created by employees of the U.S. government in their line of work, then it is almost always in the public domain. Whether you are looking for images of military tanks, super-cell tornados, bald eagles, or the Ebola virus, you're likely to find what you need. Here is a sampling of government agencies sites with searchable, downloadable, public domain images:

- National Fish & Wildlife Service

- National Oceanic and Atmospheric Administration

- U.S. Antarctic Program Photo Library

- National Institutes of Health

- The Public Health Image Library of the CDC

- General Services Administration (has links to various sources of images)

The Library of Congress (LOC) has an extensive collection of downloadable works including personal journals from the Dust Bowl, early baseball cards, Civil War maps, and historical images from the civil rights movement. However, not everything on the LOC site is in the public domain. To determine the status of an image, click on the hyperlink *Rights and Restrictions* that appears on the page with the image.

3. The work is not copyrightable.

As I discussed above, ideas, book titles, raw data, real-world events, and objective information are not protected by copyright and so are in the public domain.

4. The work was donated to the public domain through a Creative Commons license.

A creator may use the Creative Commons CC0 mark to designate a work that has been donated to the public domain. The Creative Commons has a similar mark for works already in the public domain. I explain more about Creative Commons later in this chapter.

Will Your Use Infringe?

What if you determine that the image or text you want to use is still covered by copyright? Then you need to consider whether your use of the material qualifies as *fair use*.

Fair use is defined as any copying of copyrighted material (even verbatim) for a limited purpose, such as commentary, criticism, education, or parody. Such uses may be done without permission from the copyright owner.

The line between fair use and infringement is murky. There is no set formula for determining what constitutes fair use. Much depends on the facts of the case, the aggressiveness of the copyright owner, and the temperament of the judge. There is no specific number of words that may be used without permission. Non-commercial or educational use is not 100% safe, particularly if you use a substantial part of the original material. Giving credit to the author does not make a difference—you could be infringing, but not plagiarizing.

The flip side of fair use is you may have to tolerate others using your work without permission. You cannot prohibit someone from using portions of the work for criticism, no matter how nasty. You may have to tolerate parody even if it is offensive and distasteful.

In the United States, courts take four factors into consideration in determining whether a use is fair use. No one factor controls; they are weighed against one another.

1. The purpose and character of the use. Is the use commercial or for commentary, criticism, or educational purposes? Does the new work offer something above and beyond the original? The buzzword is transformative, meaning it has been altered significantly to add a new meaning or reach a new audience.

2. The nature of the copyrighted work. Is the original work factual or artistic? Reusing factual content is more likely to be fair use, while reusing artistic elements is not. Using unpublished works is less likely to be fair use due to the potential negative effect on the market value of the original work.

3. The amount and substantiality of the portion used in relation to the copyrighted work as a whole. The more you use, the less likely it will be considered fair use, especially if you use the "heart" or "essence" of a work.

4. The effect of the use upon the potential market for, or value of, the copyrighted work. If you are reducing the value of the original work, your use is unlikely to be fair use.

For example, if you use lyrics from Bob Dylan and Eminem to compare their treatment of women, that is probably fair use. But using the same lyrics in a novel to evoke a setting or to trigger your character's epiphany is not fair use and could be considered infringement.

Using a historical photo as a small part of a larger, expressive work such as a memoir or novel is likely to be fair use. In contrast, reproducing and selling the image as a poster and on mugs would not be fair use since the image is central to the product.

Fair use applies only to copyrighted work. The portions of any work that are not subject to copyright—titles; objective information such as historical facts, data, and test results; ideas; and concepts—may be used regardless of fair use.

Fair use is a defense. If you are sued, you would have the burden of proving fair use. And the court cases are not entirely consistent. The safest course is to get permission from the copyright owner. Even if you are well within safe lines, the copyright owner might sue you anyway. Think of the attorney's fees and the time involved. While I admire those who take on David-Goliath fights, I'd rather spend my time writing my next book.

Getting Permission

By now, you have internalized the warnings: don't use content plucked off the internet without permission. Suppose you find an image, lyrics, or a song you want to use, and you have determined it is not in the public domain and your use is not fair use. How do you find the copyright owner and obtain permission?

You also need to consider how many layers of permission you need. If you want to use a photograph of a painting on your book cover, you may need permission from (i) the painter of the original painting, (ii) the photographer who took the shot of the painting, (iii) the museum or owner of the painting, and (iv) the model who posed for the painting. If you want to use a song in your book trailer you may need permission from the composer, the songwriter who wrote the lyrics, and the singer and band who recorded the song. In most cases, the original composer, songwriter, and performer will no longer own any rights; they will have licensed them to one or more music companies.

Confused? You are not alone. I get so many requests from people asking how to get permission to use images and lyrics that I have written two downloadable guides to explain the process, including sample permission request letters.

- How to Use Eye-Catching Images Without Paying a Fortune or a Lawyer
- How to Use Memorable Lyrics Without Paying a Fortune or a Lawyer

You can find these guides on the Resources page of my website (http://helensedwick.com).

To search for copyright holders of other works, start with the website of the U.S. Copyright Office (https://www.copyright.gov/records/). Their online records go back as far as 1978 and include books, music, films, sound recordings, maps, photographs, art periodicals, and newspapers.

Searching pre-1978 records is awkward, and the information may be incomplete. Try the U.S.

Copyright Office's Catalog of Copyright Entries (https://archive.org/details/copyrightrecords). If you find the date of the original copyright registration, then search the records for the 27th and 28th years later to see if the registration was renewed. The entries are in alphabetical order by creators' names.

You can also have the Copyright Office conduct a search for you. Their current rate is $200 an hour.

Commercial services such as Copyright Clearance Center (CCC) and Publication Rights Clearinghouse (PRC) will also assist you in obtaining licenses and permissions. Many freelance editors also offer copyright research services or have contacts with freelance researchers.

Once you identify the rights holder, contact them and ask for permission. Your tone should be business-like with a touch of personality and creativity. You want the rights holder to buy into your vision and enthusiasm. But make sure you cover the business basics as well. Here is a sample permission request letter for images.

Dear _____ [the photographer, artist, publication, museum, or other rights holder]:

I am writing to ask permission to use _____ [identify image] on a non-exclusive basis as a _____ [describe intended use, such as cover image, featured image, within a website and/or blog post, etc.] for _____ [describe type of publication, such as print book, ebook, blog post, newsletter, logo, posters, etc.].

I believe that you are the holder of the copyright in this image. If you are not the current copyright holder, I would greatly appreciate any help you can provide to help me locate the current rights holder.

[Describe your project, such as a self-published book, a memoir, etc. Show your passion for your project and their image.]

My first run printing will be _____ copies. /OR/ I will be distributing the print book through a print-on-demand provider. I request permission to print up to _____ books, [Make this is a realistic number, such as 5000 books. If your sales take off, you *can ask for more later.] I will also be distributing an ebook. The price of the print book will be $_____, and the price of the ebook will be _____, although I may discount those prices.*

I am distributing the book in English, [mention any other languages] in the worldwide market.

I will also use the image on my website and blog. [Describe current traffic levels.] I do/ do not post third-party advertising on my website.

I request the right to modify, reproduce, display, and publish the image for the purposes described above.

I would use the image starting on _____ [date] with no known end date.

I would be happy to provide you copies for approval and upon distribution.

Please let me know if you have the authority to grant the permissions outlined above as well as the license fees involved. If you would like me to provide attribution or credit, please tell me how you would like the credit to read.

Thank you for your attention to my request.

Sincerely,

[Your name, contact info, website, social media links, and anything else that demonstrates who you are and your vision.]

Orphan Works

Recently, I had lunch with a writer who is deep into revising her memoir. She showed me a stack of photos from her years in summer stock theater, including posters, publicity photos, and actors' head shots. Unfortunately, I put my lawyer hat on and asked her if she had permission to use the photos. Most likely a photographer or theater company owns the copyright in those photos. Her jaw dropped. "How am I ever going to figure that out?"

Good question.

When the ownership of a copyrighted work is unknown, or the owner cannot be found, we have what is called an *orphan work*. Orphan works include everything from World War II photographs to anonymous internet postings. Tens of millions of orphan works are hidden in libraries, museums, and historical societies, not to mention attics. Many, such as films by long-defunct production companies, are disintegrating because no one has an economic incentive to preserve materials that cannot be displayed without risking copyright infringement. In fact, some experts estimate that 90% of all copyrighted works are orphan works.

The problem is getting worse. Many copyright laws no longer require registration and notices, making rights holders harder to find. Repeated extensions of the copyright term gave rights to creators who were already long gone. To make matters worse, the mass digitization of library and museum collections has made millions of orphan works discoverable by anyone with an internet connection.

Does a writer take the risk of publishing orphan works without permission, or must this valuable, informative work remain tucked away and inaccessible to the public? There is no right answer, but there are ways to understand and minimize the risk.

Who Are the Heirs?

If the photo or letter was created by your direct ancestor, such as a grandparent or great-grandparent, you may be an heir to the copyright in the material. If there was a will, that might dictate who inherited intangible rights, such as a copyright interest. In most cases, there was no will, or assets were left to the surviving spouse and descendants. After a few generations, that could be dozens of people.

If you are one of the heirs, then you may use the old photos and letters without permission from any other heirs. Actually, any of the heirs may use the photos and letters. However, if you make income from those materials, you are legally obligated to share that income equally with all other heirs.

Suppose you want to use a family photo taken by your grandfather in 1950. Your grandfather died, leaving everything to his children. Therefore, you share the copyright in that image with all your grandfather's descendants, meaning your parent, aunts, uncles, siblings, nieces, nephews, and cousins. You do not need their consent to use the image, but if you make net income from the image, you would be obligated to share it with them.

Is Your Use Fair Use?

Generally, using a photo or letter as a small part of a larger, expressive work such as a memoir, historical novel, or nonfiction book would be considered fair use. In contrast, selling the image as a poster or on mugs would not be fair use since the image is central to the product.

Fair use is decided on a case-by-case basis, so I can't guarantee a court will agree with me. You have to evaluate the risk yourself using the four factors listed earlier in this chapter. Or better yet, consult with a trusts-and-estates attorney.

Many universities and publishers publish documents that lay out what they consider to be the "best practices" for attempting to obtain permission to use orphan works. The U.S. Copyright Office has proposed legislation to provide "safe harbor" procedures that would offer some legal protection for those using orphan works. Until such legislation is adopted, writers need to balance the benefits and risks of incorporating the orphan work in their books.

Stock Images and Music

You can avoid a lot of the headaches and risks by hiring a photographer or illustrator to prepare custom images for you. That's the Cadillac solution. The more affordable solution is to purchase a license to use stock images.

Tens of millions of photographs, illustrations, and vector images are available at online sites such as Dreamstime, iStockPhoto, Fotolia, Shutterstock, Getty Images, Pixabay, and Jupiter Images. The images are high quality and reasonably priced. Prices range from $1 to thousands of dollars, but my guess is 95% of the images cost less than $100. Images are available in different sizes and DPI (dots per inch, a measure of resolution quality). The higher the DPI, the better the clarity and resolution of the image. For your book cover, purchase a license to a large, high-resolution image, but for your website and blog an image with a lower resolution may work fine.

Many of these sites also have music clips and videos. I created the book trailer for *Coyote Winds* using stock images and music licensed from Dreamstime and iStockphoto for under $150.

Purchase a *royalty-free license*, not an *editorial license*, which has more restrictions on use. A license means permission to use. You are not buying the copyright or ownership to the image, but the "perpetual, nonexclusive, nontransferable, non-sublicensable, world-right to reproduce the image," subject to some limitations I describe below. Royalty-free is a misnomer; you are paying the royalty up-front.

Nonexclusive means others may have the right to use the image as well. For exclusive rights (if available), the sites will charge extra, but they cannot do anything about rights already granted. Many illustrators and photographers post their work on multiple sites, so buying exclusive rights from one site may not stop sales on other sites.

A number of websites offer "free" stock images. Personally, these sites make me nervous. If you read the fine print, the sites say something along the lines of *We think these images are free to use without permission of the copyright owner, but we are not sure. Use them at your own risk. We don't accept any responsibility if someone comes after you for using one of the images downloaded from our site.*

Yikes. In light of that, I would not use a free image for something as important as my book cover. Pay a little money, and get a license from one of the stock image companies. They guarantee that they have the rights to give you permission to use the images in accordance with their guidelines.

The site iStockphoto lists the following permitted uses for royalty-free licensed images, which are fairly typical:

- Books and book covers, magazines, newspapers, editorials, newsletters; and video, broadcast, and theatrical presentations and other entertainment applications,

- Advertising and promotional projects, including printed materials, product packaging, presentations, film and video presentations, commercials, catalogues, brochures, promotional greeting cards, and promotional postcards (i.e., not for resale or license),

- Online or electronic publications, and

- Prints, posters, and other reproductions for personal use or promotional purposes, but not for resale, license, or other distribution.

The typical off-the-shelf license has some limitations, although you can purchase expanded rights for additional fees.

You may not use the licensed image

- as part of a trademark or logo;

- as part of a design-template application intended for resale, such as website templates, business-card templates, electronic greeting-card templates, or "on demand" products, such as postcards, mugs, tee-shirts, and hats (you can create tee-shirts and the like for promotional uses, but not for sale);

- in a manner that is pornographic, obscene, immoral, infringing, defamatory or libelous, or that would be reasonably likely to bring any person or property reflected in the image into disrepute; or be in any way unflattering or offensive. (Use your common sense here. If you would not want a picture of you, your sister, your mother, or your child manipulated a certain way, then don't do it); and

- in any manner that looks as if the model or person is endorsing the product, unless you say it is a model.

Some sites permit you to use the image an unlimited number of times. Others set a limit of 249,999 or 499,999 printed images and unlimited internet images. If you distribute over 249,999 printed copies of your book, bookmarks, postcards, and other materials, then you need to buy an extended license. I hope every reader of this book has that problem!

You cannot sell, transfer, or permit someone else to use the licensed image other than someone you hire to use the image for your benefit, such as a website designer or cover designer.

One problem of using stock images is the compelling image on your cover could pop up on dozens of other books. The image of the coyote on my novel *Coyote Winds* appears on at least two other books. But for a $35 licensing fee, that's to be expected.

Creative Commons

Creative Commons (https://creativecommons.org/) is one of the best innovations to grow out of global interconnectivity.

Under copyright law, for a copyright holder to grant others, such as publishers and filmmakers, the right to use copyrighted materials, licenses are granted on a one-by-one basis. Traditional copyright law does not provide a practical way to permit wide-ranging use of copyrighted work.

Creative Commons is a non-profit organization that has developed a set of off-the-shelf licenses for use by copyright holders who wish to make their work widely available for limited or unlimited purposes.

There are currently six basic Creative Commons licenses, each with its own icon, set of rights, and limitations. Creative Commons also provides an icon for designating that a work has been donated to the public domain with "No Rights Reserved."

How Do Writers Use Creative Commons Licenses?

As the licensor. To put the world on notice that a certain expression, let's say your blog, is available for copying and modification, mark your blog with the appropriate Creative Commons mark. The Creative Commons site has a simple questionnaire to help you determine the correct license (Commercial, Noncommercial, ShareAlike, etc.). Wikipedia uses the Creative Commons Attribution-ShareAlike License.

As a licensee. If you are searching for images, content, or other expression for your use, the Creative Commons site provides links to some of the larger databases for images and other content, including Flickr, Al Jezeera, Wikipedia, and the White House.

Since there are various Creative Commons licenses that provide different permissions, look at the icons carefully and read what is and is not permitted. Choose the license that covers all your intended uses, such as commercial and derivative. Your blog may be primarily informative and educational, but if you also provide links to Amazon or other sellers of your book, your use may be considered commercial. You'll always want to provide attribution to the creator of the content you're using. The Creative Commons site provides guidelines.

One warning about using Creative Commons images containing people or featuring another copyrighted work, such as a painting, poster, or sculpture: you have no reliable way of determining whether the photographer obtained releases from the people in the image or permission to use the underlying art. Do not rely on the Creative Commons license if there are recognizable faces or artwork in the image.

If you want to use an image showing a person, then create your own (with the appropriate releases) or purchase a stock image from one of the larger companies. They provide an assurance that the appropriate releases and permissions were obtained (and, in addition, they have deeper pockets to pay for lawsuits should they be wrong).

Using Public Domain Works

You do not have to limit your use of public domain works to an occasional quote or image. You may reuse entire story lines and characters as well. Books, settings, characters, and stories in the public domain are a rich source of material for writers. *West Side Story* is a retelling of *Romeo and Juliet*, and *A Thousand Acres* by Jane Smiley adds modern tensions to *King Lear*.

On the legal side, however, many writers are tentative about basing their stories on public domain works. Will they own any copyright in the work or will it remain in the public domain? The answer is a little of both. If you create new work that incorporates materials from a public domain work, you own a copyright interest in the new material; the rest remains in the public domain.

For example, when filmmakers release yet another *Midsummer Night's Dream*, they own the copyright to the costumes, sets, and all other new creations, but not Shakespeare's words. When Helen Fielding transformed Jane Austen's work into *Bridget Jones's Diary*, her new material was protected by copyright, but not the underlying story lifted from Austen's novel. No one can revive the copyright on Mr. Darcy or Lady Jane by casting them in a new light. The same with Dracula, King Arthur, Huckleberry Finn, and the Cheshire Cat.

If you are going to base a story on a public domain work, go back to original public domain work if possible. Don't base your story on another writer's retelling or the movie version, since those are likely to mix copyrighted and public domain material. If you are using a translation, do not use the specific language of the translation (which may be covered by copyright in some countries) and stick to the larger components such as the story line and characters. Similarly, don't use any illustrations, commentary, and annotations added since 1922, since those may also be protected by copyright.

Don't be fooled by bogus copyright notices. If you pick up a print copy of *Pride and Prejudice*, you are likely to see a copyright notice in the name of the publisher along with the usual statement *"No part of this publication may be reproduced."* Many of these notices are bogus; the publisher cannot claim any copyright on a public domain work.

Using Trademarks

Suppose your main character shoplifts Sephora cosmetics, slipping them surreptitiously into her Gucci handbag. Or your young hero downs Red Bulls while showing off spins on his FatBoy BMX.

Many writers use trademarks as a shorthand way to reveal a character's status, tastes, and vanities. Will using trademarks get me into legal hot water?

The good news is you have a lot of leeway to incorporate trademarks into your work.

What Are Trademarks?

A trademark is commonly known as a brand name. It identifies as particular product or service from a particular maker. A Big Mac is a trademark that identifies a hamburger from McDonald's while a Whopper is a trademark for a burger from Burger King.

A trademark is different from a copyright. A copyright applies to an expressive work as soon as the work is put into tangible form; it's automatic. In most cases, a copyrighted work may not be copied or used without permission from the creator.

In contrast, a trademark doesn't exist until it is used in connection with the sale of a product or service in the market. Trademarks may be used by writers (and anyone else) as long as the use (i) doesn't confuse buyers, or (ii) doesn't tarnish or disparage the trademark.

Confusing Buyers

The use of a trademark is considered infringing if it is used in a way that confuses buyers as to the maker of the product or provider of the service. When you walk down the streets of New York, you'll see street vendors hawking "Rolex" watches and "Ralph Lauren" shirts. They want buyers to believe they are selling the Real McCoys are bargain prices. Their use is classic trademark infringement.

But using a trademark to add detail and nuance to a fictional story is not infringement. It's hard to image a case where a writer's use of a trademark to describe a character or a setting would lead a reasonable book buyer to believe that the book was published by the trademark owner.

Using a trademark in a title could be a problem if it creates confusion. I wouldn't use a trademark in a title without consulting with someone familiar with trademark law.

Tarnishing the Trademark

Writers are more likely to get into legal trouble by using a trademark in a negative or offensive manner.

A 1970s case about the pornographic movie *Debbie Does Dallas* is a colorful example. The movie, its posters, and trailers featured a buxom star wearing a uniform strikingly similar to those worn by Dallas Cowboys Cheerleaders. Not surprisingly, the owners of the Dallas Cowboys Cheerleaders were not pleased. They sued the movie producers, claiming the film and its publicity tarnished the reputation of their trademark uniform. They won.

To avoid potential claims, writers should not use trademarks in a disparaging manner. You are asking for trouble if your characters are poisoned by a Pepsi or run over by a self-driving Tesla. Yes, you may get away with disparaging statements if your work is clearly a parody or if the statements are true. Otherwise, drop the trademark and make up a new one.

Generic Uses

Writers should also avoid using a trademark as a generic word. Trademark owners fight hard to keep their brand names from "going generic" as happened to aspirin, cellophane, and ping-pong. Instead of saying your character googled the address, say she used Google to map the route.

Finally, don't worry about marking a trademark with a TM or R in a circle. Owners of trademarks use those marks to remind the public not to use the trademarks as generic words. Writers do not need to use those symbols. They would simply clutter up the page.

Using Work by Others Checklist

- ☐ Determine if the work is protected by copyright or is in the public domain.
- ☐ Assess whether your use could be considered fair use.
- ☐ Determine whom and how to ask for permission to use the work.
- ☐ Limit the risk of using orphan works.
- ☐ Investigate low-cost options for images and text, including stock-image companies and Creative Commons licensed material.

CHAPTER FOUR

USING REAL PEOPLE IN YOUR WRITING

IN 1979 *PENTHOUSE* magazine carried a humorous piece about a Miss Wyoming whose talent performance involved a sex act that caused a man's entire body to levitate off the floor, all while she twirled her baton.

The real Miss Wyoming, Kimerli Pring, sued, claiming the article was defamatory and had made her life miserable. She felt raped by men's eyes, and she lost students from her baton twirling classes. (I am not making this up.)

A local jury awarded her $26,500,000. Her lawyer boasted that publishers like Penthouse "can no longer drape themselves in the American flag and scream freedom of the press, while smearing little helpless people for profit."

However, on appeal, the higher court reversed the ruling. It determined the article was not defamatory. Really? Wasn't the article untrue, and didn't Ms. Pring suffer?

The laws of defamation and privacy try to balance the interest of the individual against society's interest in promoting free speech and discussion. As with any area in which the law tries to balance interests, it is a mess. The statutes vary state by state and country by country. Scholars have written enough commentary to fill a small library, and they still disagree. Case rulings are inconsistent and arbitrary since they reflect the values and attitudes of local judges and juries and not the black-letter law.

And because the cases typically involve allegations of criminality, infidelity, promiscuity, paternity, or idiocy, the emotions are explosive.

There is good news, however. Considering the hundreds of thousands of books published each year, there are relatively few defamation suits. Claims are difficult and expensive to prove. Most targets don't want to call attention to a matter best forgotten. Typically, lawsuits occur only when big egos and deep pockets are involved.

However, writers need to be aware of the legal risks, particularly memoir and nonfiction writers. If you are self-publishing, you may be prepared to accept the risk, but if you enter into a publishing agreement (whether traditional or with a self-publishing provider), you will be agreeing to indemnify, defend, and hold the other party harmless from any claim of infringement, defamation, invasion of privacy, and a whole host of other "horribles." In plain language, if these companies are named in any lawsuit based upon your writing, you must hire and pay the attorneys to defend them, and you must pay their costs and damages if you lose or settle.

While I can't predict what is 100% safe or 100% unsafe, I do provide common-sense guidelines below. Be smart about risks. Take the ones that are important to your narrative arc and minimize those that are not.

What Is Safe?

- You may write about a person in a positive or neutral light. For instance, you don't need permission to thank someone by name in your acknowledgments, or to mention non-controversial information about a person, such as the name of your fifth-grade teacher.

- You may use historical names to establish context. If you are writing a memoir about the summer of 1969, you may mention Neil Armstrong and the moon landing or talk about your crush on Cat Stevens or Grace Slick.

- You may speak ill of the dead. Claims of defamation and privacy die with a person.

When to Start Worrying?

When you are publishing information about identifiable, living people, and that information could seriously embarrass them, damage their reputations, or subject them to public hatred and scorn, then you need to consider the risks of *defamation* and *invasion of privacy*. I am not talking about portraying your mother-in-law as bossy; I am talking about portraying your mother-in-law as a drug dealer.

The other category of risk is called the *misappropriation of the Right of Publicity*, namely using someone's likeness or life story for advertising, promotional, or commercial purposes.

The following information summarizes United States law. The laws of other countries, particularly Great Britain and France, are more favorable to the targets of defamatory statements.

Defamation

To prove defamation, whether *libel* for written statements or *slander* for spoken ones, a plaintiff (whom I will call "the target") must prove *all* the following elements:

False Statement of Fact

If a statement is true, then it is not defamatory no matter how offensive or embarrassing (although the writer may have violated the target's right of privacy, a topic I discuss below).

Opinions are not defamatory, even if they are vicious. If you post a restaurant review stating a meal was so bad you gagged, you will probably be fine. But one restaurant critic was sued for saying a stringy steak tasted like horsemeat. The plaintiff claimed the reference to horsemeat was a statement of fact and not a colorfully stated opinion.

Couching something as an opinion is not bullet proof. Courts see no difference between "Joe is a pedophile" and "in my opinion, Joe is a pedophile." The test is whether the statement can be proven objectively. If so, then it may be seen as a statement of fact and not an opinion. For instance, a tweeter was sued for calling someone crazy and won the case because whether someone is crazy can't really be proven or disproven. The more precise a statement, the more likely it will be considered a fact. So in the case of Joe, it's better to say "Joe gives me the creeps" or "I would never let him babysit my children."

Satire and hyperbole are not defamatory as long as the absurdity is so clear no reasonable person would consider the statements to be true. That is the key to the Miss Wisconsin reversal. The appeals court explained that since it was impossible for Miss Wyoming's sexual act to cause levitation, the *Penthouse* article cannot be seen as a defamatory statement of facts. That's how satirical publications such as *The Onion* and *MAD* magazine get away with what they print. Entertainers like Rush Limbaugh rely on hyperbole. Their statements, while vicious, are so extreme the courts assume the average reader and listener does not believe them to be true.

Identifiable, Living Person or Company

A defamatory statement must contain sufficient information that would lead a reasonable person (other than the target) to be able to identify the target.

For example, Andrew Greene has sued Paramount Pictures for $25 million claiming he was defamed by the character Rugrat Kiskoff in the movie *The Wolf of Wall Street*. Greene claims he is easily identifiable because Rugrat, like Greene, wears a toupee. In fact, Greene seems particularly offended that the toupee is "accentuated and mocked in an egregiously offensive manner."

Frankly, the film producers were asking for trouble by using something as distinctive as a toupee since it is so clearly connected to a living person. But a toupee, particularly a bad one, must have been too funny to resist.

Typically, the target must be a living *person*, but companies have sued for defamation, particularly when the damaging statement is about food. Many states have passed "Ag-Gag laws" to protect local farming interests. Oprah Winfrey was sued by a group of Texas ranchers after saying she had sworn off hamburgers because of mad cow disease. (Oprah won the case.)

Publication or Dissemination

If one person (other than the target) reads or hears a defamatory statement, that is sufficient to support a lawsuit. Nowadays, a single tweet can be heard around the world, so proving publication is easy.

Reputational Harm

A false statement must be more than offensive, insulting, or inflammatory. Portraying someone as a jerk of a boyfriend, or an insulting mother-in-law, or an obnoxious boss is not defamation. The target must show the statement "tends to bring the subject into public hatred, ridicule, contempt, or negatively affect the business or occupation of the subject."

Certain statements are assumed to cause harm. These include statements attributing someone with dishonesty, criminal conduct, association with disfavored groups such as drug cartels, a physical or mental disease or disability, sexual promiscuity or perversion, impotence, or professional incompetence.

You never know what some people consider harmful. Donald Trump sued a publisher for underestimating his wealth. In the Greene (toupee) case, the plaintiff was managing a criminal enterprise. I don't see how his professional reputation could have been harmed any more than it already had been.

Actual Malice for Public Figures

If the target is a public official or a public figure, and the statement relates to the arena in which he or she is in the public eye, then the target/plaintiff must prove the statement was made with actual knowledge that it was false or with a reckless disregard for the truth. The standard is high; the defendant/writer must have had a reasonable basis to know the statements were false. Actual malice may also be shown if the defendant refuses to publish a retraction after being shown the original statements were false.

Negligence (Non-public Figures)

Historically, if you made a false and defamatory statement against a private individual, you would have liability even if you took every reasonable precaution to determine its veracity. In recent years, courts are requiring some measure of fault or negligence on the part of the defendant. For this reason, keep good records of your research and sources in case you ever have to provide evidence that you took reasonable efforts to verify the truth of your statements. Retain interviews and copies of relevant materials.

Make sure you have your names right. If you report true facts about Robert Paulson, but carelessly type it out as Robert Peterson, Mr. Peterson may have a claim against you.

Don't try to hide behind attributing false statements to someone else or using fudge words like "it has been reported that…" You could still be liable for repeating the defamatory statement if it was unreasonable for you to rely on the source. Do your homework. Fact check. You could be held liable for repeating a defamatory statement.

Some people try to avoid liability by posting defamatory statements anonymously. With enough money and technology, they are typically found out.

Invasion of Privacy

Even if you publish the truth, you may still be sued for invasion of privacy. The law recognizes four types of invasion of privacy:

- Unauthorized disclosure of private facts;

- Physical intrusion upon a person's seclusion, such as breaking into a home, recording someone with a hidden camera or microphone, or obtaining private information through hacking or other wrongful means;

- Portraying someone in a *false light*, such as using a photo of a young man in an article about street gangs that wrongfully implies the young man is a gang member; and

- Misappropriation of the Right of Publicity.

Let's look at the first bullet point above. The long definition is *the unauthorized disclosure of private facts, about an identifiable, living person, that are highly offensive to a reasonable person of ordinary sensibilities, and are not of public interest.*

Quite a mouthful.

A target (the person filing the lawsuit) needs to prove all of the following elements in order to win a case. Four out of five won't do.

Unauthorized Disclosure

Obviously, the safest way to write about real people is to get their permission in writing. If your manuscript will be traditionally published, ask your publisher if they have a preferred form. If not, find one of the internet. The broader the release, the better.

Resist giving the person the right to review and approve your work. Too often, when people see their personal information in print, they change their minds, leaving the writer with an unusable manuscript. Not good.

Of course, consent is not always obtainable or even advisable. Does this mean you can't write about people? No. You can still write about people, but be careful about the other four criteria.

Private Facts

For information to be private, it must not be widely known. Any incident that occurs in public is not private, especially now that everyone carries a smartphone. Celebrities have a difficult time claiming they have any reasonable expectation of privacy. A movie star lounging topless on a yacht a mile from shore should not be surprised that a camera with an extremely long lens is pointing her way.

Information in court documents and news reports is also not private, although there have been cases where decades-old criminal history has been considered private. If your target was convicted of a crime as a teenager but has gone on to live a law-abiding, respectable life, disclosing the earlier crime may lead to a lawsuit.

What about family secrets? Every family has certain topics that are simply not discussed, but that does not necessarily mean the information is private. No one may speak about your cousin's drinking problem, but if your cousin has a long criminal (and public) record of DUIs, then the information may no longer be private.

Identifiable, Living Person

The private disclosure must be about someone reasonably recognizable. It is not enough that the person recognizes himself; other people must be able to identify the person. For this reason, many lawyers recommend changing names and identifying characteristics about anyone portrayed in a negative light, even in memoirs. This is permissible as long as you say in your book disclaimer that names, dates, and identifying information have been changed to protect privacy.

Like defamation, the right to privacy dies with the person. However, you should consider whether surviving family and friends might still be harmed by the release of the information.

Don't forget to consider the privacy of smaller players in your work. For instance, if you are writing about a renowned playboy, consider whether you are intruding upon the privacy of his conquests.

Highly Offensive

The disclosure must be more than embarrassing; it must harm a person's personal and professional reputation. Typically, these cases involve incest, rape, abuse, or a serious disease or impairment. Sex videos have triggered a number of privacy suits.

Not of Public Interest

This is a huge loophole that favors writers. Even if the information is highly offensive, courts often decide there is no legal liability because the information is of public interest.

Public interest does not mean high brow or intellectual. Gossip, smut, and just about anything about celebrities or politicians is of public interest. The fact that a traditional publisher decides to print the material is enough to demonstrate public interest. If a blog post goes viral, that is evidence of public interest.

Frequently, courts find stories of rape, abuse, and incest to be of public interest if they are disclosed by the victims. As you can imagine, judges and juries are not sympathetic when a perpetrator tries to claim invasion of privacy.

Intrusive fact gathering will also get you into trouble. If you gather private information by hacking, wiretapping, spying, or climbing trees to see into someone's back yard, you could get sued for invasion of privacy and trespassing.

Another flavor of invasion of privacy is called *false light*. Suppose you post a photo of a criminal arrest. Jane Doe, a bystander, appears in the picture. However, if the photo creates the impression that Jane was arrested and you do not take reasonable measures to dispel that impression, Jane could sue you for portraying her in a false light.

Right of Publicity

The Right of Publicity gives a person the right to control the *commercial use of his or her name, image, voice, and life story.* Using someone's likeness, name, or identifying information for advertising, promotional, or commercial purposes, or to imply an endorsement or affiliation, may get you sued for the misappropriation of the Right of Publicity. You would be liable for damages, including punitive damages.

You do not have to be a celebrity to have a Right of Publicity. Everyone owns this right. If someone were to use your image in an advertisement, you would have a right to stop them and collect monetary damages.

Unlike defamation and privacy claims, the Right of Publicity continues after a person's death in some states and foreign countries.

The Right of Publicity is separate from copyright. Suppose you paid a photographer $1,000 for permission to use an image of Bradley Cooper on the cover of your romance novel. You would not have a copyright problem since you obtained permission from the copyright owner, but you might have a Right of Publicity problem if neither you nor the photographer has a release from the actor. Different rights, different owners.

Finally, the Right of Publicity is a claim under state law, not federal law. The laws vary state by state. In some states, the Right of Publicity dies with the person; in others it survives for up to 100 years! Since writers intend to sell their books everywhere, then someone making a claim could bring a lawsuit anywhere. So assume the most expansive law will be applied. No commercial use for 100 years after death.

The good news is commercial use is narrowly defined when it comes to the Right of Publicity. It's limited to the following:

- *Advertising.* Using a person's likeness in an advertisement violates the Right of Publicity. The same applies to using look-alikes or sound-alikes. Bette Midler won $400,000 from Ford Motors after they used a singer to mimic Midler's voice in an automobile commercial.

- *Merchandise.* Selling tee-shirts, mugs, greeting cards, and other products with unauthorized images is a commercial use.

- *Impersonations.* Impersonating a celebrity for commercial purposes can also get you in trouble. Yes, all those Elvis impersonators either have permission from Elvis's estate or are taking legal risks.

- *Implied endorsement or relationship.* Wrongfully implying that someone has endorsed your work or was involved in its production violates a number of laws. This applies to expressive and editorial work as well.

Expressive Use is permitted. Using someone's name, image, or life story as part of a novel, book, movie, or other "expressive" work is protected by the First Amendment, even if the expressive work is sold or displayed. Therefore, using a person's life story as part of a book or movie should not be deemed a misappropriation of the Right of Publicity as long as you have added significant expressive content and have not written a purely exploitive piece.

For example, the family of Billy Tyne, the ill-fated skipper played by George Clooney in *The Perfect Storm*, sued Time Warner Entertainment for using their family history for commercial gain without consent or compensation. They also complained that the actual events had been so fictionalized as to portray Tyne as inept. After a protracted legal battle, Tyne's family lost. The Florida Supreme Court determined that the film was expressive speech and not "commercial." The fact that the movie grossed more than $150 million did not change its protected status.

Courts consider the following in cases involving the Right of Publicity: is the use of someone's name, image, or life story *reasonably related* to the subject matter, and has the user added *new, transformative elements* to the work? In nonfiction, the courts also consider whether or not the subject matter is *of public interest.* Public interest is so broadly defined it covers hard news as well as celebrity gossip.

I would avoid using anyone's image on a book cover without permission. A book cover is too close to an advertisement or merchandise. If you fall into this category and really want to use an image (assuming you've taken care of copyright permissions as well), consult with legal counsel first.

Other Restrictions

Some writers are bound by other legal restrictions. For instance, as an attorney, I cannot use any confidential information about a client, even if I change the name and mask the identity. The same is true for therapists, accountants, and other professionals. HIPAA imposes strict non-disclosure rules on doctors, nurses, paramedics, and other health professionals. If you are a trustee or partner, or have a fiduciary relationship with a third party, you have a duty not to bring harm onto the other party by disclosing personal information. So don't do it.

Have you signed a confidentiality agreement? Many public figures require their gardeners, nannies, drivers, maids, chefs, and other staff to sign strict confidentiality agreements. If you breach the agreement, you could be liable for damages. I have seen agreements that give the celebrity a claim to 100% of the revenues from the publication of any material disclosed in breach of the agreement.

If you were a party to a lawsuit settled out of court, including a divorce, take a look at your settlement agreement. Most likely, it contains non-disclosure and non-disparagement clauses. You could unwind the hard-fought settlement by blabbing.

Will you be disclosing trade secrets or other proprietary information? At your job, you may learn valuable trade secrets such as formulas, marketing plans, and manufacturing details. If you disclose that information, even if it is true, you could find yourself without a job and facing a lawsuit, if not criminal charges, for stealing trade secrets. However, if you are exposing something illegal or dangerous and the action is a SLAPP, get an experienced anti-SLAPP attorney to assist you.

Don't make threats of physical violence against individuals, the government, or the President. You could be arrested, and you would find yourself on the NSA's and the FBI's radar.

Obscenity may also pose problems, depending on the local community standards.

As always, when in doubt or when threatened with a lawsuit, seek the advice of experienced counsel.

Mixing Fact and Fiction

Writers commonly take real people and events and create dialogue, scenes, additional characters, and entire novels around them. For events that happened more than 50 years ago, there is little legal risk, although some people may send you snarky comments about historical accuracy.

I am often asked whether writers may write novels that use more modern people as characters. Elvis Presley and John Lennon seem to be the favorites. Perhaps they meet in heaven or come back to life in the future. As long as your use of these public figures is part of a larger, expressive work, then your First Amendment rights should prevail over any Right of Publicity claim.

However, I suspect that if you rely too much on a living celebrity as a character, particularly if your portrayal is racy or derogatory, you might get some unwelcomed attention from some lawyer-for-the-stars. For many writers, the risk is worth it. They figure a lawyer letter, even a lawsuit, will generate huge sales. It happens.

Writing Memoir

In exploring the journeys of their lives, memoir writers inevitably delve into the private (and imperfect) lives of others. In this chapter, I have focused on avoiding legal claims, not preserving relationships. If you are writing a memoir, then you can't avoid upsetting someone. It comes with the territory. Here are some thoughts that may help minimize conflict.

Separate the writing process from the publishing process. Writing a defamatory statement does not create a legal risk; publishing that statement does. Write your memoir as honestly as possible without feeling inhibited by the legal issues. Fear of getting sued is a form of self-editing and will interfere with the exploratory and healing process of memoir writing. After you finish a draft (or two or three) and *if* you decide you want to share the work with others, then edit with legal risks in mind. At that point, it will be easier to identify which information may be deleted or modified without losing the essence of your story.

Watch your motives. Do you secretly want your ex-spouse, boss, parent, or mother-in-law to recognize themselves in your work? Will changing one letter in a name protect you? Probably not. Publishing a memoir is not a chance to get even with somebody by skewering them like a voodoo doll. A memoir is about you, the writer, not the person who hurt you.

Acknowledge that memory is imperfect. In fact, no one remembers events the way you do. People reconstruct the past, particularly trauma, in vastly different ways including complete denial. Discuss what you remember with others who were involved, even if (or especially if) their memories differ from yours. You may gain a better understanding of yourself and your past.

Remember that accuracy and truth are not the same things. Strive for truth, even if you don't get the facts entirely correct. Be willing to change names and other identifying information to protect privacy and your own wallet. Tobias Wolff, in his memoir *This Boy's Life,* points out, *I have been corrected on some points, mostly of chronology. Also my mother claims that a dog I describe as ugly was actually quite handsome. I've allowed some of these points to stand, because this is a book of memory, and memory has its own story to tell. But I have done my best to make it tell a truthful story.*

Finally, try not to lose sleep over what other people will think and say. I hear from writers that people don't recognize themselves, and that more people seem to be upset when they are *not* included in a book. Many writers find that if they research with diligence and write with insight, they end up with a book that is closer to the truth, both factually and emotionally. That truth mutes, or at least offsets, the criticism.

As Ann Lamott said, "You own everything that happened to you. Tell your stories. If people wanted you to write warmly about them, they should have behaved better."

Getting Consent

The best way to avoid legal problems is to get consents and releases whenever you can, particular if your work is substantially based on a person's life story. Most publishers, and virtually all film producers, won't seriously consider a work based upon a life story unless consent is obtained. As more money is invested in bringing a work to life, the less risk publishers and producers want to accept. Get into the practice of getting a signed release before you record or interview someone. If you are using letters, diaries, photos, or other materials created by others, get permission to use the materials for both copyright and privacy reasons. But resist giving anyone the right to approve the final manuscript, or, like many writers, you may come to regret it.

The M.E. Factor

As an attorney, I am often asked, "Can someone sue me?" Unfortunately, anyone may sue you. Their case may not survive the first round of legal battles, but someone can still initiate and file a lawsuit even if it is frivolous.

My rule of thumb about litigation risk is the *M.E. Factor*; money multiplied by emotion. If a lot of money is involved, then a lawsuit is likely even if there is little anger or emotion surrounding the dispute. On the other hand, if someone is angry or offended, or feels threatened, then they are likely to sue regardless of a small financial stake. If you are going after Big Oil, Big Med, Big Food, Big Religion, City Hall, Wall Street, or Mr. and Ms. Big, don't go it alone. The Bigs may not care if they have a losing case. They often file SLAPP lawsuits to intimidate critics and overwhelm them with legal bills. Get a lawyer on your team early in the process, or align yourself with a public interest group such as Electronic Frontier Foundation before you publish. Also look into Media Perils Insurance.

Insurance

Your homeowner's insurance might provide coverage for defamation and privacy claims if they arise from negligence, meaning you took reasonable measures to verify all factual statements. But a homeowner's policy may not cover business pursuits, so ask your insurance agent if you should purchase a business liability policy or endorsement.

If you are writing a high-risk book, consider purchasing Media Perils Insurance. A number of organizations offer member discounts on media insurance policies: The Authors Guild, Independent Book Publishers Association (IBPA), National Federation of Press Women, National Writers Union, Publishers Marketing Association (PMA), and Small Press Center. Even with discounts, expect the annual premium to cost between $750 and $3000, depending on the scope of the coverage.

The beauty of insurance is that the insurer hires and pays the attorneys and any settlement or damage awards up to the limits of your coverage. This is why paying for insurance makes more sense that paying to operate as a corporation or LLC.

However, most insurance policies won't cover a claim if you knew your writing was false, defamatory, an invasion of privacy, or infringement. Insurance is not a get-out-of-jail-free card for intentional wrongdoers.

SLAPP and Anti-SLAPP Laws

If you speak out on a matter of significant controversy involving well-financed interests, you may find yourself the target of a *SLAPP*. A SLAPP (Strategic Lawsuit Against Public Participation) is a lawsuit filed with intent to censor, intimidate, and silence critics from exercising their First Amendment rights. The most common form of SLAPP is a defamation claim.

Journalists and bloggers are hit with SLAPPs for exposing truthful information, albeit unpleasant, illegal, or embarrassing. We can assume the plaintiff who filed the suit expects to lose the case, particularly if the information is verifiable, but the goal is to silence the offending speech without stepping into a courtroom. Of course, SLAPP plaintiffs do not admit such motivations. The defendant (perhaps you) must put up a fight to expose these motives. How many writers can afford expensive and drawn-out court battles?

Many states have passed anti-SLAPP laws that entitle a successful defendant to recover attorneys' fees, but you would have to prevail in court, which could easily take years.

If you are threatened or hit with a lawsuit that seems motivated by spite or intimidation, seek legal counsel immediately. Your rights and your wallet are at risk.

If You're the Target

What if someone posts false statements of fact about you that harm your reputation? Immediately ask for a retraction, and if that does not work, consult with an experienced attorney. But before you sue, ask yourself whether suing will only call more attention to a matter best forgotten.

Using Real People Checklist

☐ Don't say someone is criminal, sexually deviant, diseased, or professionally incompetent; or use labels such as crook, cheat, pervert, or corrupt. Instead, stick to verifiable facts and your emotional responses. *Show, don't tell.* Let your readers come to their own conclusions.

☐ Memories are subjective and evolve over time. Verify your memory by conducting research and interviewing others. Retain records to support your statements.

☐ Rely on publicly disclosed information, such as court documents and news reports wherever possible.

☐ Wait until your targets have passed away. (Okay, most of us don't want to wait.)

☐ Consider altering names, places, and identifying characteristics so targets are not identifiable to the average reader. The more villainous the character, the more changes you should make. The same is true if you are using a company as an evil character, such as a polluter.

☐ Watch your motives. If you are writing a getting-even book, write the manuscript with passion, and then put it aside for months, even years. With time and perspective, you will be better able to mask your characters and make the story more universal.

☐ Ask yourself how important the information is to your narrative arc. Judges and juries can be moralistic and will punish someone who discloses private information gratuitously or maliciously.

☐ Consider using a pen name and hiding your identity. The people in your book may be less recognizable if readers do not know there is a connection.

☐ Get releases and consents from recognizable people appearing in your work whenever possible.

☐ Don't use anyone's image for advertising and promotional purposes without express permission.

☐ Add disclaimers. I give some samples in Chapter Ten.

☐ If accused of a defamatory statement, consider publishing a retraction.

☐ Engage an attorney to review your manuscript.

☐ Always reach for the truth when writing—it's the best defense.

If you have not noticed by now, I recommend avoiding lawsuits, even if you have done nothing wrong. Litigation and arbitration are more risky and unpredictable than you realize. And the process is expensive and incredibly stressful. You are better off spending your time and energy promoting your book and writing the next one.

CHAPTER FIVE

PEN NAMES

IF YOU ARE a surgeon, you may not want your patients to know you crank out thrillers with high body counts. If you dabble in bondage fiction, you may wish to hide that tidbit from nosy neighbors, straight-laced employers, and your church group. The more edgy or controversial your work, the more you'll be tempted to hide behind a pseudonym.

I am often asked if using a pen name is legal. Will a writer be accused of identity theft and fraud? Will he or she be sued by using the name of a real person?

Using a pen name is completely legal. In fact, it is often a wise choice. But one caveat about using a pen name—it will make your life more complicated.

Before you decide on a pen name, consider whether you can achieve your purposes by using your initials and your last name, or your middle name or nickname and your last name. Using a variation of your real name is not considered a pen name, so you don't have to go jump through the usual hoops or deal with the typical complications. Joanna Penn (thecreativepenn.com) uses this method. She publishes her nonfiction books under the name Joanna Penn and her novels under the name J.F. Penn.

Why a Pen Name?

Privacy. Privacy is one of the main reasons writers choose pen names. In particular, memoir writers want to explore family secrets, yet still be invited to holiday dinners. Many writers report that they feel freer to write under a pen name.

Branding. Writers often choose pen names to support their literary persona, be it mysterious, authoritative, or lovable. They may have different pen names for different genres. A writer with an audience in romance will choose a different pen name for a dark, dystopian fantasy. Writers who have bombed under one name start over with pen names.

Changing genders or ethnicity. Similar to branding, pen names may be used to create a new persona for personal or marketing reasons.

Avoiding confusion. I recently co-wrote an ebook with Jessica Brown, and we discovered there are at least three other Jessica Browns selling books on Amazon. If a writer has a common name, or the same name as someone famous, a pen name avoids confusion.

Ease of reading. Today, people shop for books by scanning online thumbnails instead of browsing bookstore aisles. Writers are selecting short pseudonyms that pop from the screen, particularly if they have long names that are difficult to spell.

Collaborations. Two or more co-writers might pick a single name for publication.

Choosing a Pen Name

Choosing a pseudonym can be as daunting as naming a character, especially since the character is you. The simplest pen name would be a variation of your own name, such as a middle name, nickname, or initials. Many authors change only their last name so they don't have to remember what first name to use at conferences.

Once you decide on a list of possibilities, do the following:

- *Research.* Search the internet and bookselling sites. Avoid any name already used by a writer, since that is likely to confuse readers. Do not use the name of anyone famous. If you write a book under the pen name Taylor Swift or Derek Jeter, you may be accused of trying to pass yourself off as the celebrity. I also suggest a trademark search through the U.S. Trademark Office. If you use the name of registered trademarks, you risk getting a cease-and-desist letter. Try to avoid using the name of a real person. If you happen to use the name of a real person, you are not committing identity theft. Identity theft involves intentionally acting to impersonate someone for financial gain. But if your writing affects the real person's life, consider changing your pen name.

- *Buy available domain names.* You will want to buy a domain for your pen name.

- *Claim the name.* File a Fictitious Business Name Statement (FBN Statement) if you will be getting payments made out to your pen name. (I explain how in Chapter Eight.) In some jurisdictions, you may have to add the word *Books* or *Publications* after your pen name because the local jurisdiction won't accept a Fictitious Business Name that looks like the name of a real person.

- *Use the name.* Place the pen name on your cover and your copyright notice: © *2017 [your pen name]*. Some authors put the copyright notice in both their pen name and real name, but it is not necessary.

- *Be open with your publisher.* Usually, you will not be able to hide your real name from your publisher since contracts are signed in your real name. The exception is when you form a corporation, LLC, or other entity (as I describe in Chapter Eight), but even then, most publishers want to know their authors.

- *Register your copyright.* You may register the copyright of your work under your pseudonym, your real name, or both. There are downsides to registering the copyright under a pseudonym only. First, it may be difficult to prove ownership of the work at a later date. Second, the life of the copyright will be shorter: 95 years from the year of first publication or 120 years from its creation, instead of 70 years after your death. I recommend that authors register their pseudonymous works under both their real names and pen names. This creates a permanent record of ownership, and few readers are going to research copyright records and find out the author's real name.

There is no way to "claim" a pen name as exclusively yours. You may go through the process of filing an FBN Statement, but that gives you the right to use that name, not the right to stop others from using the same name (unless they happen to be doing business in the same county as you). If you become very famous under your pen name, then you might have other options. If that happens, you should engage a lawyer to help you.

What Not to Do

- *Don't go overboard in creating a fake identity.* Never claim credentials you don't have. Using made-up credentials, especially to market an advice book, would be a misleading business practice.

- *Don't use a pen name to avoid a pre-existing contract.* If you have granted a traditional publisher first-refusal rights or have signed a confidentiality agreement as part of a legal settlement or employment agreement, a pen name won't change anything. You are still breaching your obligations.

- *Don't expect a pen name to protect you completely from defamation claims.* Most likely, you will be found out either through legal process or technology.

Licensed Professionals

Using a pen name for a book containing professional information may not be permitted by the rules of your license. For example, the American Bar Association and the California State Bar would consider this *Handbook* a "client communication" and "advertisement." Therefore I *must* disclose my real name according to ethical rules. If I were writing a novel, I would have more freedom to use a pen name because readers are not relying on my legal credentials.

Secrecy

You should consider how secret you want to be about your true identity. Maintaining secrecy is difficult. The higher the level of secrecy, the more complicated the process. Plus, you need to keep track of which identity to use in what context.

Most authors choose to be open about their pen names. At book signings, they use their pen names, but at writers' conferences they use their real names with a reference to their pen names. For example, Dean Koontz lists his various pen names on his website.

Some authors are more discreet. They try to maintain their privacy, but not to the point of lying. They don't put photos on their books and blogs, do not link their websites, and limit public appearances. For a bio, they use their own life story, but told in generic terms. David

Savage (a pen name) did that with his bio for his book *How the Devil Became President* (http://howthedevilbecamepresident.com/).

Other authors put up roadblocks. They set up corporations and trusts to hold the copyrights and contracts. This is the most expensive alternative and may require an attorney. Even then, someone will know who is behind the corporation, and word may leak out. In this internet age, secrets are almost impossible to keep. Remember what happened to J. K. Rowling? She tried to keep quiet about her pen name Robert Galbraith, but it was leaked by, of all people, her lawyers.

Pen Names Checklist

- ☐ Consider using a variation of your own name, such as a middle name, nickname, or initials.

- ☐ Choose an easy-to-read name that fits your brand image.

- ☐ Research the market to see if any other writers are using that name.

- ☐ Buy the domain name for your pen name.

- ☐ File an FBN Statement to claim your name and so you can accept payments in that name.

- ☐ Decide how much secrecy you want to maintain.

CHAPTER SIX

MAKING THE BOOK

NOW COMES THE big question—HOW?

How do I self-publish?

How do I turn my manuscript into a print book and ebook?

How much will this all cost?

At this point, the self-publishing process may seem daunting, confusing, impossible. It's not, as long as you approach it one step at a time. You have accomplished harder tasks, such as driving a car, passing a school exam, and writing a book.

There are scores of books and websites that can walk you through the technical details of preparing your manuscript and launching your book much better than I can. I list many of them at the end of the *Handbook* under Resources. In this chapter, I will give you an overview of the self-publishing pathways and help you avoid costly mistakes.

Offset vs. POD

I am assuming that you will be using a print-on-demand (POD) process to produce your books instead of traditional offset printing. Offset printing is preferable for a work requiring precise, high-quality printing, paper, and ink, such as a photography or art book, but it is too expensive for print runs of fewer than 500 copies. Few self-publishers use offset printing.

POD books are produced one copy at a time using high-end laser printers, which is cheaper for small print runs. You will have various options for trim sizes, but few choices about paper or binding. POD books are not as high quality as books produced with offset printing, but they are higher quality than the mass-market paperbacks you find at grocery stores.

The POD process is flexible, which is important for an indie author. You might tweak (or entirely redo) your cover, title, and interior contents if sales (or reviews) indicate that revisions are warranted. POD printing is an affordable way to try new looks and approaches a few copies at a time. After all, who needs 1,000 outdated books languishing in the garage next to the abandoned stair climber?

Self-Publishing Service Companies vs. DIY

You have two main pathways for converting your manuscript into a print book and/or ebook:

- *SPSC.* Engage a self-publishing service company (SPSC) to do everything from editing to distributing your book. BookBaby, Dog Ear Press, and Mill City Press are SPSCs.

- *DIY.* Do it yourself by hiring editors, designers, and other professionals and then uploading your print-ready files to a print-on-demand (POD) provider such as CreateSpace and/or IngramSpark and your ebook files to various ebook distributors such as Smashwords, Draft2Digital, Kindle Direct Pubishing (KDP), and iBooks.

You may also mix the two approaches, since most SPSCs have a la carte menus, and many DIY providers offer editorial, design, and marketing services as add-ons.

And there are so-called hybrid publishers. They operate like an SPSC in that they charge writers for editing and design services. But they purport to share the up-front investment in return for a percentage of royalties and the exclusive right to sell your work for a period of five to ten years.

You could hire a self-publishing consultant or coach to walk you through the process. Literary agents are also jumping in and offering to manage the self-publishing process for writers—for a percentage, of course.

How do you decide which option is right for you?

Self-Publishing Service Companies (SPSCs)

At first, almost everyone is tempted to hire an SPSC because the DIY process involves hundreds of decisions. What's the best trim size? What colors will make your cover pop? What font conveys the correct tone? How do you price your book? What do you say on the back cover? How do you hire the right editor, designer, or publicist, and what if you have to fire them?

In contrast, SPSCs promise to deliver books into your hands in a few weeks, although at a higher price than the DIY option. I heard one speaker describe the DIY option as camping and the SPSC option as staying at a hotel.

Dozens of SPSCs offer hundreds of self-publishing packages that include editing, design, distribution, and marketing services. The packages start at a few hundred dollars and run as high as $35,000. Some SPSCs are Abbott Press, Blurb, Book Baby, BookLocker, Dog Ear Publishing, Lulu, Mill City Press, Outskirts Press, and Xulon Press. The notorious Author Solutions runs AuthorHouse, Balboa Press, CrossBooks, iUniverse, Palibrio, Trafford, WestBow Press, and Xlibris, among others.

In the past, people referred to SPSCs as *vanity presses*, but vanity presses work on a different business model. Typically, they require authors to buy large quantities of their own books, often at inflated prices. Vanity presses are still out there; Morgan James is one. Although they don't charge authors high fees for editorial, design, or distribution services, they require authors to purchase 2,500 copies of their own book at the cost of printing plus $2.00. So if the cost of printing is $4.00 per copy, the author will pay out $15,000 and will need the space to store all those books. Since the term *vanity press* has become pejorative, many SPSCs now call themselves *subsidy, co-op, equity,* or *entrepreneurial* presses.

Today, SPSCs work on a new model. They make their money by (i) selling services to writers (often terribly overpriced), and (ii) selling writers copies of their own books (often at inflated prices). SPSCs do not make money from selling your book to the public. They make money from selling services and copies of your book to you.

Selling services is not a bad thing. As a lawyer, I sell services. But I have a problem when anyone convinces writers to buy services they don't need, such as Hollywood screenplay packages costing $10,000 to $20,000. Or a company farms out editing to non-English-speaking editors who can't spell. I am not making this up.

Some SPSCs pretend to be traditional publishers. They require writers to "submit" manuscripts for consideration. While they may be weeding out obscene or defaming work, they accept almost every submission. Having your manuscript "accepted" is flattery intended to loosen your wallet.

The simple way to distinguish between a traditional publisher and an SPSC is to look at which party is making the financial investment in editing, design, production, distribution, marketing, and promotion. As soon as the so-called publisher asks for your credit card number, you should know you are dealing with an SPSC.

I'll admit that I am on a bit of a rant. I get calls and emails from people (typically elderly and vulnerable) who have been talked into buying tens of thousands of dollars in services from these SPSCs. And others who see that their books have reasonable Amazon sales ranking, but the SPSC never pays them a dime. Not all SPSCs are unscrupulous; many are quite honest and professional. But you need to be careful.

Here's my simple approach for assessing an SPSC—how much will your book cost for readers and for you?

Price? Isn't that putting the cart in front of the horse? What about editing and design? Print quality? Getting on store shelves? They matter, but only if your book is competitively priced.

The harsh reality is that most of your sales will be through three channels: ebook (predominantly Kindle); online through Amazon, Barnes & Noble.com, etc.; and sales you make yourself at author events and through your website. Your book is unlikely to be carried by brick-and-mortar stores no matter how well executed. The stores won't sacrifice shelf space to an unknown author. Even *Fifty Shades of Grey* and *The Martian* broke out first as ebooks.

Some SPSCs set the retail price for your print book unrealistically high. One company claims its high pricing is author friendly because it increases potential royalties. Forget it. You may have a fabulous book, perfectly edited, with a stunning cover, but if it is priced at $20 alongside bestsellers priced at $15, $12, or $8, few people will buy it. To market your book successfully, the price must be competitive. I would stay away from any SPSC that will price your book out of the market.

Choose an SPSC that will sell you copies of your books at a reasonable author price. As an indie author, you will be selling books directly at readings, school visits, and conferences, and through your website. You will also give away dozens, maybe hundreds, of copies to reviewers, bloggers, friends, and family. Overpaying for these books will swallow your profit.

The author price should be the actual printing cost plus a reasonable markup (15–20%) and not a discount from the retail price. Why pay more for copies of your own book because the SPSC sets the retail price at $18 instead of $10? The printing costs are the same. You have already paid the SPSC hundreds, if not thousands, of dollars for design, editorial, and marketing services. You deserve better.

As of this writing, the Author Solutions companies set the retail price of your book (unless you pay extra!). Suppose they price your paperback at $19.95, and then offer to sell you copies at a 30% discount. You will pay $13.96 per copy, plus another $2 to $3 for shipping and handling. That's two to three times the actual printing cost.

According to Mark Levine's *Fine Print of Self-Publishing*, the cost for POD printing of a 250-page, 6" x 9", black-and-white trade paperback on standard paper is $0.015 per page plus $0.90 for a color cover, so $4.65 per copy. I went to the websites of various SPSCs to determine whether they would set the retail price and if they charged high markups on author copies.

AuthorHouse fixes the retail price at $19.99, and the author price is $13.96 per copy for orders of 24 or fewer copies.

Dog Ear Press does not fix the retail price, and its author price is $6.28 per copy.

Mill City Press (owned by Levine) does not fix the retail price, and its author price is $4.60 per copy.

CreateSpace does not fix the retail price, and its author price is $3.85 per copy.

This is a significant spread and worth calculating before choosing any SPSC.

Other Criteria:

Author-friendly website. Be wary of any company if its website does not provide an easy way to calculate the price of publishing packages, optional add-ons, royalties, retail pricing, and the author price (assuming different options such as page count). If the website states that pricing, royalties, and such cannot be determined until your manuscript is reviewed or formatted (and typically after you have given them your credit card number and paid a nonrefundable amount), move on to another website and another company that promotes transparency and author control.

Honest sales practices. Steer clear of any company that forces you to talk to a live person to get basic information. If you prefer to talk to a live person, that's great, but you should not be forced to endure a sales talk to get the basics. And once they get your phone number, they will call you repeatedly, sometimes for years! These guys are pros at separating you from your money. Call to ask questions, but if they launch into a sales pitch, warn them you will hang up if they don't stop immediately.

Avoid any SPSC that engages in bait-and-switch tactics. If a self-publishing package is listed at $399 online, but by the time you include basic add-ons the price jumps to $1,399, forget it.

Easy termination. You should have the right to terminate the relationship following not more than 30 days' notice delivered via email. None of this *certified mail, return receipt* nonsense. After termination, the provider may have the right to sell off its existing inventory, but that's it. It should not have the right to continue to print and sell your book, even if such rights are nonexclusive. If a traditional publisher were interested in your work, they would want to (or want you to) buy out your former SPSC before they penned any deal with you.

Delivery of production files. If you terminate your relationship with an SPSC, then it should deliver to you the final production files of your cover and interior at no or low cost. Not PDFs of your print-ready files, not digital files, but the actual, functional production files in Adobe InDesign or comparable format. It is outrageous for an SPSC to hold onto these files after you've paid for the design, editing, and layout work. You own the work product. They cannot reuse it.

Easy-to-calculate royalties. As I mentioned earlier, be suspicious of any company that does not have a royalty calculator on its website. How can you compare one company against another if you cannot compare potential royalties?

Reputation. Research the reputation of any provider before you sign up. Some SPSCs have good reputations; others do not. For instance, Author Solutions and its various companies have been hit with lawsuits claiming breach of contract and illegal sales tactics. You don't have to spend a lot of time doing the research; other people have done that for you:

- Alliance of Independent Authors maintains a rating system and list to help distinguish between the good and the bad service providers (http://selfpublishingadvice.org/allis-self-publishing-service-directory/self-publishing-service-reviews/).

- *The Fine Print of Self-Publishing* by Mark Levine, now in its sixth edition, compares the packages, costs, pricing, markups, and contracts of SPSCs and POD providers in detail.

I have read authors' complaints about SPSCs inserting typos into books, and then charging the author to make corrections, not once, but repeatedly. Every company will have its share of unhappy customers, so sort through the complaints to try to get a sense of which ones are legitimate. If you find multiple reports from unhappy customers, stay away.

Do your homework before you commit.

Doing It Yourself

Despite any first impression, the DIY process is manageable if you take it one step at a time. Instead of hiring an SPSC, you engage your own team and act as your own publisher, similar to being your own general contractor for a home remodel. If you are on a tight budget, you could do much of the design and layout work on your own or through trades with other writers and designers.

I use the DIY option.

POD and ebook distributors, such as CreateSpace, IngramSpark, and Lightning Source for print books and Smashwords and Kindle Direct Publishing (KDP) for ebooks, focus on the DIY self-publisher.

To use a POD and ebook distributor, you and your team create print-ready and ebook-ready cover and interior files meeting the technical specifications of each site, for example, size, DPI (dots-per-inch, a measure of clarity and resolution), and file format. You upload the files, and the POD and ebook distributors take care of the rest.

Potentially, your earnings will be higher if you go the DIY route since you are not paying the SPSC its profit. You'll have control over design, timing, pricing, discount rates, costs, and the production files.

Bu now, the journey of transforming your project from manuscript to print book and/or ebook now seems less like an impassable mountain road and more like a well-worn path. You are retaining control of your work and your dream. You are growing from writer to author.

In the next chapter, I'll walk you through finding, hiring, and working with your publishing team. Most of these professionals are a pleasure to work with because they love what they do.

Making-the-Book Checklist

At this point, you have decided between the SPSC and DIY processes or crafted a combination of the two approaches. You have

- ☐ chosen an SPSC that permits you to control retail pricing and discount rates, charges a reasonable price for author copies, returns production-ready files, and has a user-friendly, informative website and fair contract terms, or

- ☐ elected the DIY route and are ready to engage and manage your own publishing team.

CHAPTER SEVEN

HIRING FREELANCERS

UNLESS YOU ARE amazingly talented or have a collection of generous and gifted friends, you will need a team to transform your manuscript into a book.

With the downsizing in the publishing industry, plenty of top-notch editors and designers are available for freelance projects. Prices will vary widely. Remember the most expensive editor, designer, or publicist may not be the best person for you or your book. But the cheapest may be a greater waste of money. Look for relevant professional experience, good word-of-mouth references, and an aesthetic style that fits your own.

Meet Your Team

Editor. There are different levels of editorial review ranging from developmental editing (structure and plot) to copyediting (detailed, line-by-line editing). The Bay Area Editors Forum website has a handy explanation of the different editing options and has a search function for finding editors. The fee for an editor may vary from $500 to $5,000 and up, depending on the length of your manuscript, the editor's experience, and the editorial options you choose.

Copy editor. A copy editor checks grammar, punctuation, and consistency. Do not rely on friends. They won't be nit-picky enough. Communicate with your copy editor about whether you want a light, medium, or heavy copyedit. And make sure to ask if your copy editor's fee includes proofreading. Some copy editors do not proofread unless asked. The fee for a copy editor ranges from $0.015 to $0.050 per word. Some charge by the hour, typically $35 per hour and up.

Cover designer. A good cover catches the reader's eye and communicates the theme of your book. Most designers have sample covers on their websites. Many offer ready-made templates at reasonable prices. If you are working on a tight budget or accelerated time frame, ready-made cover templates are an attractive option. Fees range from $10 (for a template) to $5,000 for a custom illustrated cover.

Interior designer for print books. The designer selects fonts, chapter headings, and other design elements, and lays out each page. Fees range from $200 to $2,000. To do your own formatting, check out the design templates at BookDesignTemplates.com. Those run between $50 and $100.

Website and blog designer. Cost will depend on the number of pages as well as how many bells and whistles you want. Fees range from $50 to $5,000. You can do this yourself if you have the patience. Maintaining your website and email will cost you between $100 and $150 per year, again depending on size and number of features.

Conversion/formatter for ebooks. If you are publishing a novel without unusual formatting, then you can convert your manuscript into an ebook fairly easily. If your book contains charts, graphs, and photographs, or has special formatting requirements, then you are better off hiring an expert. Typically, the cost is between $50 and $200. No matter which route you follow, check your book in each format (Kindle, iPad, etc.) as text that looks fine in one version may be chopped up in another.

Photographer. Do not have your spouse take a photo of you in the backyard with the dog. Do not hold your phone at arm's length for a selfie. A headshot session is fun. Get dressed up. Be a character. Be glamorous. Be both. You have worked hard on this book, and now is your moment to shine. Fees for professional photographers range from $200 to $400.

Social media consultant. There are experts who will help you set up your social media presence, including coaching you on how to use time-management and analytic services such as HootSuite, Twylah, Socialoomph, and Social Report. They write posts and tweets for you and can help you choose keywords and content to improve SEO. (SEO, *search engine optimization,* increases the likelihood that your site or blog will rank high in internet searches.) Fees are usually on a per-hour basis, ranging from $50 to $150 per hour.

Publicist (optional). Look for a publicist with a track record in your genre—the more focused the better. A generalist is likely to put in thousands of dollars of effort with no tangible result. Fees for a freelance publicist can start at $1,000 and go much, much higher.

Finding the Right People

Your goal is to find freelance talent with real-world publishing experience within your genre. Don't hire a self-help editor to revise a historical novel or a racy romance artist to design the cover for a book about grief.

Here are resources for building your team:

- Joel Friedlander and Betty Kelly Sargent have put together an amazing resource book titled *The Self-Publisher's Ultimate Resource Guide.* The book lists selected editors, designers, book shepherds, printers, teachers, publicists, marketers, workshop leaders, illustrators, reviewers, and other professionals. It includes useful articles on everything from formatting to press releases.

- The Alliance of Independent Authors (http://allianceindependentauthors.org/services-directory/) is building a database of vetted service providers for independent authors.

- Reedsy.com is developing a curated database of professional editors, designers, and marketers. According to their website, they are selective and list only 3% of the professionals who apply. You can search by specialty, such as romance or sci-fi.

- Ask for recommendations from authors, including traditionally published ones. Find books in your genre and email the writers. Many will respond with information and advice.

- Check with local writers' groups and organizations, particularly any organization of independent publishers.

- Post questions on writers' forums and communities.

- If you get in touch with one freelancer who isn't a good fit, ask for a referral. There's a network of good people out there.

- Online sites such as 99cents Designs, Elance, Freelancer, and VoiceRealm match up freelancers and projects, often by a bidding system. You'll get offers from freelancers worldwide. They will range from rank beginners to seasoned professionals. These sites act as go-betweens for handling payments and approvals.

You will also find designers, editors, and other potential members of your creative team by searching online for "book cover designer" or "book publicist," etc., but read the websites carefully. Be wary of any site that boasts the company "knows the market" or "knocks down doors" or "turns your rough draft into a diamond," but says nothing about the freelancers' work experience. Look for credentials. Don't hire a rookie with a slick website.

Contract Basics

Suppose you have chosen an editor, cover designer, interior designer, photographer, illustrator, audio book narrator, or other freelance contractor. Now what? How do you spell out your mutual expectations or, to put it in legal language, the *terms of engagement*?

Your freelancer may have a form agreement that is no more than a description on a website or an email. These are acceptable forms of contracts and will form binding agreements even if they are 100% electronic. However, *make sure the agreement covers the following items*:

What services are expected. Spell out what you expect the contractor to provide. For example,

- line-by-line editorial review for a 80,000-word novel. Describe the project's genre, such as thriller, romance, historical novel, memoir, how-to, or travel book;

- complete copyediting for grammar, typos, and continuity, including proofreading;

- internal layout for a specific trim size and/or for an ebook in a list of electronic formats;

- a specified number of rough cover designs, number of revisions, final design in print-ready PDF format and/or Adobe InDesign files;

- website of x number of pages, images, tabs, links; banners for Facebook, Twitter, etc.;

- timing of deliveries;

- number of revisions included in price; cost of additional revisions; and

- format of final product.

Payment. Is the payment refundable in whole or in part if you are not satisfied? Are there any ongoing payments such as royalties or renewal fees? Any expense reimbursements?

Attribution. Are you required to give the freelancer attribution, for example, "Cover designed by XYZ," "Audio book narrated by GHJ," or "Photographs by ABC"?

Credits. May the freelancer list you as a client on his or her website? Post your cover, illustration, or photo on the website? You should clarify whether the freelancer must hold off posting your cover until your book is launched.

Termination. Either party should have the right to terminate the agreement at any time. If the engagement is not working out, either one of you should be entitled to bail out. It's better to lose some time and money than to stick with a relationship that is not working.

Many freelancers include a "kill fee" in their agreements: if you change your mind and terminate the contract before the work begins, you agree to pay a fixed amount, typically 5 to 10%of the total contract price. This compensates the freelancer for booking you into his or her schedule. A reasonable kill fee is fair.

Communication. What is the preferred method of communication? Is the freelancer available for telephone calls? Is there a limit on the number of calls?

Rights. Your agreement should say the following:

- The freelancer represents and warrants that he or she has the authority to transfer the final product to you free and clear of any claims of any third party.

- If the freelancer has used anyone else's intellectual property, such as stock music or images, the freelancer has obtained all permissions and licenses necessary to permit you to use them.

- The freelancer's final product (such as illustrations and designs) is exclusively yours. However, if your design incorporates stock images from a site such as Shutterstock or a free image available to anyone through a Creative Commons license, then you will not have exclusive rights to those stock and free images.

I recommend that you not use the phrase *work-for-hire*. It is a shorthand expression for a complicated set of legal rules. If you use the expression without understanding it, you may be in for some unpleasant surprises. In California, if you use the term *work-for-hire*, the freelancer is considered an employee and you are considered the employer unless your freelancer is a corporation, LLC, or other entity. Therefore, you are responsible for unemployment insurance, workers' compensation insurance, and income tax withholding.

Here is a sample of a general assignment of intellectual property rights:

> *Effective upon my payment of $_____, you assign and transfer to me the Work Product and all rights, title, and interest in and to the Work Product and all versions,*

derivatives, and revisions, whether now in existence or to be created in the future, including all copyrights in all languages, in all known or unknown forms, media, or means of expression, all rights to display, perform, reproduce, modify, merchandise, trademark, or otherwise commercially exploit the Work Product. You acknowledge that evolving technology may result in the development of new media and means of expression and exploitation of the Work Product, and agree that this assignment and transfer shall encompass expression and exploitation of the Work Product in all media by all means whether now known or invented in the future.

Many people are afraid to hire freelancers. What if they hire the wrong person and have to deal with the awkwardness of firing them? Get over it; it's going to happen. Here are some suggestions for minimizing the risk of having to part ways:

Be clear about your expectations and standards up-front. If you don't know what you want, then don't hire someone until you do. You are much more likely to get frustrated with your freelancer (and vice versa) if you can't articulate the services, styles, tone, design, etc., you want. Take the time to consider your options; look at samples; and write out your goals, likes, and dislikes before you hire someone.

Don't accept sloppy or substandard work. If you are not happy with someone's work, take the time to figure out why and articulate your expectations. Most professionals appreciate the opportunity to make their work better. Even if they grumble behind your back, you will get a better work product and more respect.

Admit your mistakes. If you signed on with the wrong freelancer, admit it and find a way out, even if it costs money. Everyone makes mistakes. I've paid for cover designs I never used and wasted money on worthless promotions. Sometimes you just pay the piper and move on.

Tax Reporting

Remember the Nanny Tax—all the buzz about failing to report payments to babysitters and gardeners that brought down some Presidential appointments? Well, you won't risk public humiliation if you fail to report payments made to editors, cover designers, website designers, publicists, or others, but you could face costly penalties. Plus, you'll pay higher taxes. I cover the tax issues of hiring freelancers in Chapter Eleven.

Hiring Freelancers Checklist

☐ You have chosen a team of professionals with relevant experience who fit your style and budget.

☐ You have discussed the details of the engagement including scope of work, timing, pricing, refunds, and attribution.

☐ You have put that agreement in writing or email.

CHAPTER EIGHT

BUSINESS SETUP

"I have questions on how to set up the business end. If I choose XYZ Publishers as the name of my publishing business and then want to take credit cards and write checks, those will read XYZ Publishers. But sometimes I want customers to see my name on the check or receipt. Would I need two business credit cards? Two checkbooks? Two business licenses? Should my EIN number be under publisher or author name? What forms do I fill out to be a sole proprietorship? Some people tell me I'm crazy not to form a corporation. Help!"

MOST INDIE AUTHORS, like the one who wrote the email above, are confused by the alphabet soup of EINs, DBAs, LLCs, and 1099s.

Here's a little secret. Setting up your business is one of the easier parts of self-publishing. The process is a series of steps, many of which are as simple as filling out the right forms at the right time. Taken in the right order, you can set up your business in a day. Or, if you are adopting a business name, a day and a half.

Before I get started, let me explain why it makes sense to approach self-publishing as a business.

Why Operate as a Business?

Our tax code encourages people to start new businesses. In fact, the IRS expects businesses to lose money at first, so the tax code provides tax breaks to help offset early losses. If you are publishing independently with the goal of making money, then you are entitled to enjoy these tax benefits like any other entrepreneur.

The key is to operate as a business and *not* as a hobby.

If your writing and publishing activities are considered a *business* by the IRS, then you may deduct writing-related expenses from non-writing income. In contrast, if the IRS considers your activities to be a *hobby*, then you may deduct writing expenses from writing income only. This can cost you real dollars.

Suppose you spend $5,000 hiring editors, designers, a formatter, and a publicist to develop and launch your book. At the end of the year, you make $1,500 in gross sales. You may deduct $1,500 of your expenses from the $5,000 of income whether your writing is considered a business or a hobby. But you may deduct the remaining $3,500 of expenses from your "day job" income only if you are operating your writing and publishing activities as a business, and, if audited, can demonstrate that to the IRS.

You may have heard the old rule that the IRS considers a business to be a hobby unless the business shows a profit during three out of five years. In practice, the hobby rule is not as strict as the three-out-of-five-year rule. A business does not have to be profitable, but there must be a realistic expectation that it will earn a profit. And you must be able to demonstrate a serious intent to operate the business at a profit.

Occasionally, I hear from writers who are nervous about calling their writing endeavors a business and deducting writing expenses from other income, at least until they are making a small profit. That's fine. This tax strategy is not mandatory. But you will still be better off if you set up your business properly. You will need an EIN and a Seller's Permit—and to deal with 1099s and W-9s, even if your writing never grows into a profitable business.

Now let's get down to business.

Incorporate or LLC?

If you mention you are going to be self-publishing a book, then your brother-in-law, neighbor, or some other busybody is going to say that you must incorporate or form a limited liability company (LLC) in order to protect your assets.

Smile politely and ignore them. They are wrong, at least 95% of the time.

For the vast majority of writers, forming a corporation or an LLC is an unnecessary expense, easily hundreds of dollars a year. And it doesn't do them much good. A writer's greatest legal risks are defamation, privacy, and infringement claims, all of which result from the writer's personal actions, not the acts of the entity. Even if a writer forms an entity, someone would sue both the writer and the corporation or LLC.

I operate as a sole proprietorship for both my legal practice and my self-publishing business, even though it would take me 15 minutes to incorporate. There's no need. There are better options, namely insurance. If you are really worried about defamation, privacy, and infringement claims, consider buying Media Perils Insurance. I cover insurance below.

If a business is not a corporation or LLC, then what is it? A *sole proprietorship*.

A sole proprietorship may be owned by you alone or by you and your spouse. You do not have to file any documents with governmental entities to create a sole proprietorship. You do not need to give your sole proprietorship a business name, although I recommend that you do. You create a sole proprietorship simply by going into business.

A sole proprietorship is not taxed separately. You will report its revenue and expenses on a Schedule C, which is attached to your 1040 and the equivalent state tax form.

The vast majority of small businesses operate as sole proprietorships. According to the Tax Foundation, in 2014 there were more than 23 million sole proprietorships in the United States. They are simpler to operate and subject to fewer arbitrary rules than C corporations, S corporations, and LLCs.

If you are combining efforts to produce and share income with one or more other people (other than your spouse), then you are forming a general partnership. The partnership is created as soon as the partners agree to combine efforts to earn a profit. Your agreement may be verbal, but I recommend you capture it in writing. The process of writing down a partnership or collaboration agreement forces the partners to discuss issues they may be avoiding.

Already incorporated? Maybe you have already formed a corporation or LLC. No problem. You have not made a mistake. If the cost of maintaining the entity in your state is low, then you might as well keep it in existence. It serves as one more indication that you are operating your writing as a business for tax purposes. But if the annual fees in your state are more than you want to spend, consider dissolving the entity.

Are You One of the 5% Who Should Incorporate?

Consider the 4 Ps.

- Privacy

- Profits

- Partnership

- Protection

Privacy. If you want to hide your identity, you can use a pen name, but that's not a perfect solution. At some point, CreateSpace and other providers will ask for your real name. The more people who know your real name, the more likely the information will leak. For an added layer of privacy, form a corporation or LLC and publish and register your work in the entity's name. Even then, you must designate a living person (other than you) to sign corporate documents. That person should be your attorney, accountant, or someone you trust. All this costs money, probably $500 to $1,000 a year depending on where you live. For some people, it's money well spent.

Profits. If you expect to make making significant income from your writing, let's say $50,000 or more a year (some accountants say $100,000 or more), then it may make sense to form an entity to save on self-employment taxes.

Partnership. If you run various businesses with different partners and investors, then you may want to set up an entity to distinguish one business from another.

Protection. If you are writing a high-risk book, then you may want the additional layer of protection of operating as an entity. A high-risk book is one that takes on Wall Street, City Hall, Big Business, Big Data, Big Medicine, Big Agriculture, Mr. or Ms. Big, or any other target with the money to hire a pack of lawyers to make your life miserable. Setting up a corporation or LLC is beyond the scope of this *Handbook*. There are many sites, services, and books to help you. However, you will be better off working with an attorney or CPA. It's far cheaper to set the entity up correctly in the first place than to clean up a mess later on.

Setting Up Your Business

Setting up your business is a two-step process.

- In the first step, you will come up with and claim your business name (optional), including filing a Fictitious Business Name Statement (FBN Statement) and obtaining various business numbers and certificates (EIN, Seller's Permit, etc.).

- In the second step, you will use a certified copy of your FBN Statement to open bank accounts. Then you will link those accounts to CreateSpace, IngramSpark, and other vendors and retailers.

I suggest you take the steps in the sequence laid out below. That way you'll have the right information when you need it and will minimize backtracking.

Naming Your Business

Even if your self-publishing business is a sole proprietorship, I recommend you give the business a company name, commonly known as a DBA, short for "doing business as." Your company name will also be your imprint name, and you will list it as the "publisher" of your book online, in catalogues, and on the book itself.

Some writers are confused by the idea of operating under a DBA name. Isn't that the same as setting up an entity?

No. A DBA is merely another name for you. I am known by various names: Helen Sedwick, Ten Gallon Press, and to some people Mom or Aunt Helen. But all of those names mean me.

Your company name is different from a pen name.

- A pen name is listed as the *author* of your books.

- A company name is your *imprint name* and is listed as the *publisher* of your books.

The traditional justification for choosing an imprint name was to mask that a book was self-published. Many bookstores, reviewers, bloggers, contests, and readers refused to consider self-published work. The taint of self-publishing has greatly diminished over the last few years as more indie authors earn high sales and great reviews. But I still recommend adopting a business name because it encourages you and others to see the venture as a business.

Be forewarned that some bloggers criticize self-publishers for using imprint names by claiming they are misleading readers into thinking their books are traditionally vetted and published. Hogwash. Think of all the small businesses you know: the local flower shop, the wedding photographer, the physical therapist, the fruit seller at the farmers market. Many of them are sole proprietorships that use DBAs. Why not you? Your self-publishing venture is no less legitimate a business.

Choosing a company name is a creative process. Optimally, the name will imply some promise about your books, such as romance (Passion Press), adventure (Kick-Ass Books), travel (Rickshaw Riders), or life-changing insights (Next Chapter Publications). My novel *Coyote Winds* is set in the American West, so I chose Ten Gallon Press as the name of my imprint. I tried dozens of other names, such as Prairie Winds Press and Coyote Publications, but I researched their availability and found they were already in use.

Your imprint name may include the word *company*, but should *not* include *corp.*, *corporation*, or *inc.*, unless you have specifically set it up as a corporation.

Don't lose sleep over choosing the perfect company name. Few people will remember the name, and it's not as important as your book title or your characters' names. But it is important to choose a name that's not already in use in the publishing or related businesses or your local community.

Using a company name that is already in use may lead to conflict if

- the name or a confusingly similar name is used by a *similar business*,

- the name is already associated with a *well-known brand*, such as Starbucks, Sears, or Apple (no brainer; don't do it), or

- someone in *your local county is using the same name*, whether or not they are in a similar business.

How do you determine if there is a conflict?

Search registered trademarks. Go to the U.S. Patent and Trademark Office (USPTO) and conduct a search. If you find a registered trademark that is the same as or similar to your name, do not despair. Most of the time, you may use a name similar to an existing trademark as long as you do not *"create a likelihood of confusion in the mind of the consumer as to the source of the product."*

What does that mean? Here's an example:

I searched the trademark "Goody Two Shoes" and found one "live" registration by MaxWax Inc., for a "hair removal service using wax or sugar that removes hair from women or men up to two inches inside the bikini line." If you named your imprint Goody Two Shoes, you are highly unlikely to be infringing on MaxWax's trademark because your products and services are so different. However, if you find your dream name being used as a trademark for books or anything related to publications, communications, or education, keep brainstorming. If you use it as an imprint name, you are asking for legal trouble.

Search your state's trademark database. As of this writing, the California Secretary of State's office will search up to two names by phone and more by mail. In other states, you may be able to search online.

However, do not use a well-known or strong trademark such as McDonald's or Exxon, even if you would be using it on a noncompeting product. Owners of strong marks have the right to challenge any similar trademark that may "dilute" the value of their trademark regardless of the product or service. Avoid this fight. Those companies have lawyers who will make your life miserable. You are better off saving your energy for writing your next book.

You are not done searching yet. Most businesses do not bother registering their trademarks with the USPTO, so search unregistered trademarks (also called common law trademarks) as well.

Search for unregistered trademarks. Search your company name using Google, Bing, and other search engines. If you find a company using the name as a trademark, apply the *likelihood of confusion* test. If the company is selling auto parts, then using the same or a similar name for a book imprint is not likely to cause confusion and be considered trademark infringement.

Also search industry-related indexes such as *Literary Marketplace* and *Poets & Writers Magazine Directory of Small Presses.*

Search domain names (URLs) on GoDaddy or other ISP sites. Searching domain names will alert you to other possible users. Again, the fact that other businesses use the name is not a problem if their businesses are not related to books or publishing. However, it would be preferable to own the domain name for your company name. If the domain name is not available, try adding other words such as *press, publications,* or *books.* Try various spellings and misspellings. See where people land if they type your domain name incorrectly.

Search your county's index of FBN Statements. Many counties have online databases. In California, I use DBAStore.com. In other states, search "searching DBAs in [name of your state or county]." Some states, like Oregon, manage DBAs on a state-side basis, not by county. Some states, like Oregon, manage DBAs on a state-side basis, not by county.

Legally speaking, you may not use a DBA already in use in your county *whether or not the businesses are different.* This is not the same as a registered or unregistered trademark where you consider the likelihood of confusion.

Although DBA laws are not generally enforced by governmental agencies, the owner of the existing business could complain and make you change your business name. It's best to use a name that is not in use within the county where you will operate your business.

For example, you want to call your imprint *Three Little Pigs.* My search of the USPTO and the internet found many other users of that name, but all related to food products, not publishing. No problem there. But suppose you find a butcher in your county with the registered DBA Three Little Pigs. Because you would be using the same DBA in the same county, that butcher could stop you from using Three Little Pigs, even though you are in different business.

Once you have decided on a company name, let's make it yours officially.

File a Fictitious Business Name Statement (FBN Statement) in the county where your business will be located. For most of us, this is our home.

In most states, you may not operate a business under a name other than your own unless you file an FBN Statement. Practically speaking, you won't be able to cash a check made out to your business name unless you have filed an FBN Statement.

Some people will call this a DBA (doing business as) filing. It's simple and inexpensive. In California, I use DBAStore.com. Everywhere else, search "Fictitious Business Name" and the name of your county. You will find services that handle the process for a small fee, typically less than $100. Handling the filing yourself won't save much money, so let the experts take care of it while you work on other business steps.

In California the filing involves (1) recording the FBN Statement with the county recorder and (2) publishing a notice in a local newspaper once a week for four weeks. Most states have similar requirements. You should renew your FBN Statement every five years.

About a month after you submit your FBN Statement, you will receive a certified copy of the statement. Keep it in a safe place. You will need it to open bank accounts.

While waiting for the FBN Statement, take care of the following:

Federal Employer ID Number

Obtain a separate Federal Employer Identification Number (EIN) for your publishing business. An EIN is equivalent to a Social Security Number for your business. Once you have an EIN, you will use the EIN instead of your social security number for all your business accounts and dealings. It is added protection against identity theft.

- You may get an EIN even if your business is a sole proprietorship and never has any employees.

- You may obtain an EIN whether you operate under a company name or your own name.

- It's free and takes about 10 minutes.

Be sure you go directly to the IRS website to apply for your EIN(www.irs.gov). The site operates from 7 a.m. to 10 p.m. Eastern time.

WARNING: Sham sites that look like the IRS site are popping up every day. They ask for your Social Security Number, mother's maiden name, birthday—all the tools for stealing your identity. Scary stuff. These sites also charge hundreds of dollars to get an EIN. Go directly to the IRS site and it's free.

Your EIN will be issued while you wait online. Print out the EIN application page and the page giving you the EIN. Save those pages with your business records. Write down your EIN someplace handy. You will need it often.

State EIN

In some states you may have to obtain the state equivalent to the federal EIN. Check the requirements for your state. In California you do not have to obtain a state EIN unless you are hiring employees.

Resale Certificate or Seller's Permit

If you will be selling books either in person or through your website, you are required to obtain a *Resale Certificate*, sometimes called a *Seller's Permit*, from your state, unless you live in one of the few states that do not charge sales tax. A Resale Certificate is different from your EIN, ISBNs, business license number, or any other number. Welcome to the number-filled world of small business!

Many states issue Seller's Permits and certificates online and/or by mail. Some states require the certificate to be posted at the place of business, although no one is going to come into your home office to inspect your bulletin board. If you don't post the certificate, then keep the original certificate in a safe place.

The good news: once you provide a copy of your Resale Certificate or your certificate number to CreateSpace, IngramSpark, or other POD provider, you won't have to pay sales tax on books *you buy with the intent to resell.*

The bad news: When you resell your books to your customers at readings and book fairs or through your website, you will be obligated to pay sales tax to the state in which the transaction takes place, although you may charge it to your buyers. And you are required to fill out state sales tax forms and pay sales tax to your state. Calculating, collecting, and paying sales tax is a headache. I will discuss more details in Chapter Eleven under Sales and Use Taxes.

Business Licenses

Many cities and counties require businesses to obtain a business license. You'll have to do your own research on this item since each state, county, and even city has its own rules. In some jurisdictions, you are required to get a business license only if you have employees. Others don't care about employees, but they ask about total sales. Generally, the larger the town or city, the higher the cost.

Do a web search for "business license" and the city, town, county, and state where your business is located. Often, a city or state website will have a section to help with this process. Check for links titled *Doing Business, Starting a Business,* or *Business Portal.*

For example, I researched the business licenses a small publisher would need if he or she worked from home in San Francisco. I learned that every person engaging in business within the city must register with the Office of the Treasurer and Tax Collector within 15 days after commencing the business and must renew the registration and pay a new fee every year. The annual fee depends on gross revenues and number of employees, but the minimum annual fee is $90. The writer must also register with the Assessor's Office, which imposes a personal property tax on the writer's business property, such as computers and printers.

Domain Names

You will find it most helpful to obtain the .com domain, but consider buying .net, .info, and other tags as well. Also, buy domains for your name (or pen name) and your book title (or alternative tentative titles). If those domain names are already taken, try adding descriptive words. For example, if my name were taken, I might try the domain name HelenSedwickwriter.com.

When you register a domain, your name, address, phone number, and email are searchable on whois.net. For added privacy consider purchasing Private Registration for your imprint domain.

If you will be taking credit cards and transacting business on your website, then purchase an SSL Certificate, which will ensure that data is encrypted. If you are processing sales through PayPal or a similar site, you do not need an SSL Certificate; they provide the encryption and security.

Purchasing ISBNs

If you plan to make your print book available to bookstores, libraries, and online retailers, then each version of your book should have its own ISBN. An ISBN, short for International Standard Book Number, is a unique identifier for a particular version of a book in a specific format. You don't need to use an ISBN for the Kindle version of your book sold through Amazon, but you will need an ISBN if you want to sell ebooks through Smashwords and many other ebook distributors.

If you can afford it, I recommend that you purchase your own ISBNs and not use the ISBNs offered for free or for a low price by CreateSpace or other providers.

As of this writing, if you use one of CreateSpace's free ISBNs, then the publisher of your book will be listed as CreateSpace Independent Publishing Platform, which is like screaming that you are a *self-publishing novice*. If you buy one of CreateSpace's Custom ISBNs for $10, then your imprint will be listed as the publisher. While this sounds like the perfect solution, you may use the custom ISBN *only* for copies provided by CreateSpace. If you use other POD providers such as IngramSpark, you may not use the CreateSpace ISBN. You will end up with two versions of your book that are identical except for the ISBNs. Both are likely to appear on Amazon and other online sites, creating unnecessary confusion.

The same is true for ISBNs you buy or get for free through most other self-publishing service companies. You will not be able to use those ISBNs with IngramSpark, CreateSpace, or other providers. You will lose that ISBN if you move your book to another printer.

CreateSpace also offers a transportable, Custom Universal ISBN for $99. That is for a single ISBN. Since you will need more than one ISBN, you will save money by buying a package of ten ISBNs directly from Bowker for $295 *in your imprint name*.

How to Buy Your Own ISBNs

Each country has its own company or agency that issues ISBNs. In the United States, all ISBNs are issued by R. R. Bowker.

There are a lot of companies that are not Bowker offering to sell ISBNs. One of them is called Publishers Services. These companies are acting as middlemen between you and Bowker and are charging extra fees. Plus, unless you read the fine print carefully, they could be listed as the publisher of your book instead of you and your new imprint name. Not good. Go to the Bowker site directly (https://www.myidentifiers.com/).

If you are using more than one POD provider for the same book at the same time, then make sure you use the same ISBN for all the POD providers. For instance, if you wanted to sell your print book on Amazon through CreateSpace (without Expanded Distribution) and through IngramSpark to reach bookstores, you would use the same ISBN with both companies.

Many experts recommend that writers purchase packages of ten ISBNs. You need one for each version of the book, each format, and every translation. You will use one ISBN for your paperback, a different ISBN for the ebook, and another one for the audio book on CDs. Here is a list of when to use a new ISBN:

Fixing typos	No
Price change	No
New edition	Yes
New cover	Yes
Ebook version	Yes, but optional for Kindle
Audio book	Yes
Hardcover	Yes
New publisher	Yes
New size	Yes
Translation	Yes
New book in a series	Yes
Excerpts and supplemental materials if sold separately	Yes

When you receive your ISBNs, print out the list. When you assign a particular ISBN to a book and version, be sure to write down the assigned book and version next to the correct ISBN; otherwise, it's easy to lose track.

ISBNs are not transferable, so do not buy an ISBN from a friend or through an advertisement. If you purchase an ISBN in the secondary market, there is a risk that the number could be canceled or that your book will be listed as published by someone else.

ISBNs are not recyclable. If a version of your book goes out of print, you may not reuse its ISBN for another version or book.

Now, take a break.

For the next steps, it's best to wait until the FBN Statement process is completed and you have a certified copy of your filed FBN Statement to show your bank.

You may decide to jump ahead and open your CreateSpace, IngramSpark, PayPal, and other accounts before you have your certified FBN Statement. That is not a problem. But once you open separate business bank accounts, update your accounts at the various sites in order to direct royalty payments and credit card charges to your business accounts.

Business Accounts

When you receive your certified FBN Statement, set up your bank, PayPal, Square, and other business accounts. Setting up separate business accounts has many benefits. With separate accounts and credit cards, the process of sorting business income and expenses from personal income and expenses will be a snap. The IRS is more likely to consider your writing a business if you maintain separate accounts and records.

Head down to your local bank branch with a copy of the certified FBN Statement, your driver's license, and your personal checkbook. You can set up an account online, but I find that doing this in person is easier. Plus, you'll enjoy seeing your local bank officer's eyes light up when you say you are there to set up a business account.

Open a basic business checking account and get a credit card in the name of your DBA. You will not be using payroll or any other services at this time, so don't let the bank talk you into opening an expensive account with services you don't need. In addition, I would not set up a merchant services account that lets you accept credit card charges through your bank. As of now, PayPal and Square are less expensive options for accepting credit card charges.

Once your bank accounts are opened, go online and open a business account at PayPal. (Yes, one that is separate from your personal PayPal account.) The free PayPal option provides enough functions for 99% of writers. Link your business PayPal account to your new business bank account and credit card.

Accept Credit Cards

You can accept credit card and PayPal payments using your smartphone or tablet by signing up with Pay Pal Here, SquareUp (often called Square), or other similar payment processing services. They will mail you these neat little gizmos that plug into or otherwise work through your cell phone and accept debit and credit cards (and soon Apple Pay and other contactless payment systems). As of the writing of this book, the fee is 2.75% (give or take) of the charge, but there is no minimum monthly fee. Your bank is likely to charge a substantial minimum monthly fee to accept credit cards with a merchant account.

Other Business Accounts

You will find it handy to set up separate business accounts with USPS, UPS, and FedEx in your company name, using your company credit card. Having separate accounts will help you keep track of your expenses, and many providers offer lower rates and better service to their business customers. Go to their websites and register under your business name, using your EIN and business credit card.

Many writers rent a P.O. box to use as their business address. That way they keep their home address more private.

CreateSpace, IngramSpark, Smashwords, and other Providers

Set up your accounts with CreateSpace, IngramSpark, Smashwords, and other providers.

- Give them your business EIN instead of your personal SSN.

- Direct your royalties to be paid into your business bank account.

- Make your business credit card your default payment method.

- Give them your Seller's Permit or Resale Certificate number so you may purchase copies of your book for resale without paying sales tax.

- IngramSpark may have you download a set of state forms to print, sign, scan, and return to them to establish your exemption from sales tax for books you buy from IngramSpark for the purposes of resale.

Recordkeeping

A few weeks ago, a client called me in a panic. He received a letter demanding $2,000 for using an image on his website without permission. My client was sure he bought the image from a stock image company, but he couldn't find the receipt anywhere. He admitted he never kept those things, because he never thought anything would go wrong.

Without decent records, the task of sorting out the mess is more difficult and potentially more expensive.

While filing is everyone's least favorite task, keeping good business records is critical for protecting your rights, getting what you have bargained for, and saving money at tax time. When it comes to tax audits, more people are penalized for losing receipts than for cheating. Don't be one of them.

Dedicate file drawers (real and virtual) to your publishing business long before your book hits the shelves. I prefer clear, plastic, stackable file boxes, since the IRS likes to see paper. Plus some business records, like your FBN Statement, sales tax permit, and copyright registration certificates, will be in print.

Keep the following:

Contracts. Retain copies of all agreements with freelancers, publishing companies, webhosts, advertising/social media companies, and POD providers as well as related correspondence, especially if the correspondence contains assurances, explanations, and special offers.

Licenses. Whenever you pay for images, fonts, lyrics, and other content, you are buying a license, which means permission to use. There are limitations and terms of use/service connected with those licenses. Print out the license (and your receipt while you're at it). Most online sites have a print-friendly version, but if not, print out the webpage showing the relevant terms or save a screenshot. Note the date the webpage was printed or saved. And of course, read it.

Expense receipts. See if you can document your expenses down to the penny!

Receipts from your own sales. Buy a small receipt book that creates duplicate receipts, and write out a receipt every time you sell a book. Note on the receipt how much was paid (including sales tax), and whether the book was hand delivered or shipped. If shipped, note the city and state the book was shipped to. I also find it handy to make out a receipt for myself when I give a book away. It helps me keep track for tax purposes, which I will discuss more under Sales and Use Taxes.

Financial records. Save bank, credit card, PayPal, and other statements.

Government correspondence. Save everything you send to or receive from the IRS or any governmental entity, including copies of every check.

Mileage log. Buy a simple calendar/planner to keep in your car. On the day you get it, write down the mileage on your odometer. From now on, write down your odometer reading on January 1 (or as soon after that date as your remember).

The IRS requires that you keep a log of all business-related miles, so every time you use your car for writing-related reasons, write down where you went and the mileage. Or use your phone to take a picture of the odometer. That records time and place.

Writing-related driving includes trips to conferences, readings, research sites, post office, and bank. I doubt it includes long drives to seek inspiration or blow off steam.

Screenshots. If you run ads on social media sites or blogs, or if you and your work are discussed, interviewed, reviewed, or featured on any website, take screenshots showing you and your work, and save them. Occasionally run a Google search of your name and books and save screenshots of several pages listing you and your work. All these are evidence that you are working hard to promote your work as a profit-making business.

Some not-so-obvious records to keep. Keep virtual or printed copies of the following to help support your position that you have been actively pursuing writing as a business with the goal of making a profit:

- Schedules from conferences you attend, particularly if you spoke at them
- Thank you notes from readers or people who have heard your talks
- Takedown notices
- Appointment books and calendars
- Business cards and manuscript critiques
- Fan emails
- Contest entries and notifications
- Correspondence with freelancers, whether or not hired
- Correspondence with publisher and agents, including rejection letters

Home expenses. If you use part of your home *regularly and exclusively* for your writing business, then you may be able to deduct a percentage of your overall home costs (mortgage, insurance, utilities, maintenance, repairs, taxes, rent). So keep everything from mortgage statements to garbage bills.

How Long Should You Keep Business Records?

Keep contracts and licenses for as long as your book is on the market. You never know when you will have to remind a designer or someone else that you did pay for an image and have the rights to use it.

Keep financial records for seven years. Some people say three, but if you are starting a business, I suggest seven years in case you have to prove to the IRS that writing and publishing is your business and not a hobby.

Business Setup Checklist

- ☐ Decide if you should form a corporation or LLC.
- ☐ Select an available company name.
- ☐ Claim your company name by filing a Fictitious Business Name Statement.
- ☐ Obtain a federal EIN and a state EIN, if applicable.
- ☐ Register for a Seller's Permit or Resale Certificate in your state.
- ☐ Register for a local business license, if applicable.
- ☐ Buy domain names.
- ☐ Set up separate business PayPal, checking, and credit card accounts.
- ☐ Register with Square, PayPal, and other services that process credit card payments.
- ☐ Set up accounts with CreateSpace, IngramSpark, Smashwords, Draft2Digital, and other services in your imprint name, using your federal EIN and Seller's Permit.
- ☐ Buy a file box or cabinet to maintain business records. It's deductible.

CHAPTER NINE

FINANCING YOUR BOOK

EDITING, DESIGN, PRODUCTION, marketing—what's this all going to cost, and how are you going to pay for it? Producing a well-edited, professionally designed book takes money, anywhere from $200 to $15,000 depending on

- whether you are publishing an ebook, paperback, and/or hardcover,

- how much you do yourself instead of hiring freelancers, and

- how many print copies you want on hand.

In addition to hiring the freelancers, you can expect to spend money on the following:

- ISBNs ($295 for 10)

- Bookmarks, postcards, business cards, and other promotional materials

- Free copies for bloggers, reviewers, media contacts, friends, relatives, your freelancers, and other writers

- Paid reviews

- Book trailers

- Advertising and promotion

- Trade shows and book fairs

- Contests

It's easy to overspend in self-publishing. After all, these books are our children, and we want what's best for them.

I have read that 95% of books (including traditionally published ones) sell fewer than 1,000 copies. Now, I hope that all my readers sell thousands of books and make back their financial investment many times over. Considering the odds, don't spend more than you can afford to lose.

Business Plan vs. Budget

You have probably heard that every writer should have a business plan. You may feel unprepared because you haven't started one (and don't really want to). My guess is 95% of indie authors never write up a business plan. Writing and publishing are giant leaps of faith. Perhaps we don't want to examine that faith too closely.

Even if you don't have a business plan, you must have a budget.

Remember the key distinction between a hobby and a business; you are able to demonstrate to the IRS that you have a serious intent to operate the business at a profit. How will you demonstrate your intent if you never put pen to paper and calculate if and when you will break even?

For an idea of the size of the market for your book, look at Amazon sales ranking for books similar to yours. Let's assume the bestselling books in your category have a Kindle sales rank of 50,000 (meaning about 5 ebooks a day or 150 a month), and a 50,000 print-book ranking (meaning about 2 print copies per day or 60 a month)—respectable numbers for an independently published book. How much in royalties will you earn each month assuming you get 70% of the retail price for ebooks and 40% for print? The number will surprise (and probably disappoint) you.

Assume the suggested retail price of your print book is $15 and ebook is $4.99.

60 copies x $15 x 40% = $360

150 ebooks x $4.99 x 70% = $523.95

TOTAL: $883.95 per month or $10,607.40 per year

Now $10,607 a year is not chump-change, but few of us could quit our day jobs and live on that.

Now ask yourself,

- How much money can you lose without affecting your lifestyle or losing sleep?

- How many more books do you have in you? (Most writers do not break even on their first book.)

If you need to live to be 110 in order to break even, see what happens if you reduce expenses or increase estimated sales. Whatever you do, don't despair and give up. Remember that you are writing and publishing for intangible rewards as well as financial ones.

When does a writer need a full-blown business plan?

- Crowd funding. A business plan is essential if you are crowd funding. Your publishing venture will not seem legitimate or thought through without one.

- Loans. If you are looking to finance your book through micro-financing, a personal loan, or an SBA loan, your lender will want to see a well-written, realistic business plan.

- Self-discipline. Think of a business plan as a partnership agreement between you, as writer, and you, as business person. What are you, the writer, going to do to satisfy you, the business person, that your publishing has the best chance at success? Think in terms of both financial and time commitment.

Going through the process of writing out a business plan, no matter how rough, will open your eyes to the possible and impossible. There are many resources available to help writers develop business plans, including Joanna Penn's *How to Make a Living with Your Writing* and *Business for Authors*.

Financing Options

Let's start off by emphasizing that paying publishing costs with credit cards is a no-win strategy. The high interest rates will eat up all your profit and then some. There are better ways:

Crowd Funding

College student Devin Mitchell started a Kickstarter campaign to fund *Veteran Vision Project*, a photography book about soldiers struggling with the return to civilian life. He promoted the book by posting his photographs on various websites. His campaign was so successful he quickly passed his $20,000 goal and raised more than $70,000.

In crowd funding, the writer seeks contributions by setting up an online campaign and asking for contributions. Some crowd funding sites also allow writers to take pre-orders.

Many websites provide platforms for pitching crowd funding projects. Kickstarter and Indiegogo are probably the most well known, but others claim to specialize in helping authors, including Unbound, Publush, Authr, and Rockethub. Some sites charge a percentage of the amount raised, while others charge a flat monthly fee. Some are based on the all-or-nothing model, meaning the author collects nothing unless a certain dollar target is achieved. Others do not have a minimum threshold, and the author keeps whatever is raised. Still others offer a choice. Some of these sites also offer additional services, such as market testing, advertising, and printing. (Watch out for the fees on the extra services.)

A new crowd-source model is being offered by Inkshares.com. Authors post their books on Inkshares.com and try to generate pre-orders. If the book generates 750 pre-orders, then InkShares provides full publishing services, including editing, design, printing, distribution, and marketing in return for a share of royalties. If the book attains only 250 pre-orders, then a smaller set of publishing services is offered.

With InkShares, as with anyone who gets their hands on your manuscript, take the time to read their publishing contract. If you get 750 pre-orders, they get the exclusive right to publish the work in print and digital formats, worldwide, in any language, plus a cut of the royalties for ten years! They also get the exclusive right to manage licensing for derivative works, such as film and merchandise. If you can generate 750 pre-orders, then you might not need them after all.

I can't repeat this enough— always read the fine print.

Crowd funding is a major project in itself. If you hope to get contributions from more than family and friends, be ready to commit some serious time and effort. You should have a professional-looking website, a compelling video, and sample pages to communicate a clear vision of what you are offering and why people should give you money to bring it to life.

Crowd funding works best for people who already have a robust virtual platform, in other words, a strong voice and a lot of followers.

A few legal points about crowd funding:

When soliciting money do not call it an investment. If you are selling an investment, then you are selling a security (like a stock or bond), which is subject to a complex array of federal and state laws. Yes, even if you are raising $2,500, you are selling securities that require registration and the preparation of detailed disclosure statements. There are exemptions from the registration requirements, particularly if you are taking investments from family and friends only and in small amounts. But if you will be soliciting funds from anyone and everyone on an online site, call the funds *contributions*, not investments or loans.

Do not say the contributions are tax deductible. Many people hear the word *donation* and assume it is tax deductible. Not the case. Unless you are a nonprofit entity that has applied for and received tax-exempt status from the IRS, your crowd-funding money is not deductible by the donor. I prefer to use the word *contribution*.

Contributions may be taxable income. From what I have read, the IRS has not yet decided whether funds raised through crowd funding are taxable income or nontaxable gifts. The more cautious approach treats contributions as taxable income because they are funds obtained in pursuit of a business venture. If you have deductions for expenses at least equal to the contributions received, you may offset this income with these deductions.

Sales tax may also apply. If you are offering to send donors copies of your book in exchange for contributions, then you are "selling" the book and owe sales tax on that sale.

Grants

A number or organizations provide grants, awards, and fellowships to writers. Here are some information sources and listings:

- *PEN America* has a low-cost listing of 1,500 domestic and foreign grants, literary awards, fellowships, and residencies available to writers in all income brackets, for work in all genres, and at various levels of achievement. (https://www.pen.org/ns-grants-and-awards)

- *Poets and Writers Magazine* (http://www.pw.org/grants) organizes listings by genre and date.

- *Funds for Writers* (http://fundsforwriters.com/) has both free and low-price subscription newsletters that list paying markets, grants, and competitions for writers, among other useful information.

Other Options

- *Advertising in your book.* Although most readers cringe at the thought of seeing advertisements in books, the practice is creeping into acceptance. We have all read print and ebooks that slip in advertisements for similar books or books by the same author. Consider inserting a few non-obtrusive ads in your book, perhaps from a cover designer in exchange for a discount.

- *Ebook only.* It is far less expensive to produce an ebook than a print book. If finances are tight, or you want to test the market before investing in the print book, release an ebook only.

- *Pre-selling from your website.* Permit people to pre-order your book from your website or as part of your crowd-funding campaign. Make sure your bookkeeping system is well oiled first. You want to keep track of all pre-orders so you can fill them when the book is released. And remember, all that money is taxable income in the year in which you receive it. So try to incur business expenses in the same tax year in which you collect money for pre-orders.

- *Small business loan.* If you have a good relationship with your bank and a strong business plan, you may be able to obtain a small business loan.

- *Gifts.* Let family and friends know that you don't want any more "stuff" for your birthday, holidays, etc., and instead you'd like contributions to your publishing fund.

Financing Your Book Checklist:

☐ Estimate your potential revenues.

☐ Create a comfortable budget.

☐ Consider drafting a business plan. The exercise alone is worth it.

☐ Prioritize your expenses. Editing first, design second, marketing third.

☐ Research sources of funds, such as crowd funding, grants, pre-sales, and gifts.

CHAPTER TEN

DISCLAIMERS

MANY AUTHORS ASSUME the legal disclaimers at the front of their books are supposed to be boring. They presume some pricey lawyers devised standard legalese, and they dare not depart from the norm.

Not so.

The law does not require a disclaimer to be boring. In fact, the opposite is true. The more interesting the disclaimer, the more likely it will be read. From a lawyer's point of view, a well-written, well-read disclaimer is best of all.

Many writers have a lot of fun with their disclaimers, particularly for memoirs. Let's look at a few.

Fiction

Every reader is familiar with the typical fiction disclaimer. *This is a work of fiction. Names, characters, businesses, events, and incidents are the products of the author's imagination. Any resemblance to actual persons, living or dead, or actual events is purely coincidental.*

I find nothing wrong with this disclaimer, except that it won't work in many instances. What if your novel includes real events, places, and historical figures? What if parts of your book are based on your own life? Let's take a look at how some authors have dealt with these issues.

Tom Wolfe in *A Man in Full* acknowledges that parts of his story are from real life: *This novel's story and characters are fictitious. Certain long-standing institutions, agencies, and public offices are mentioned, but the characters involved are wholly imaginary.*

Margaret Atwood in *Cat's Eye* tries to dispel the reader's assumption that the book is the alter ego of the writer: *This is a work of fiction. Although its form is that of an autobiography, it is not one. Space and time have been rearranged to suit the convenience of the book, and with the exception of public figures, any resemblance to persons living or dead is coincidental. The opinions expressed are those of the characters and should not be confused with the author's.*

A disclaimer can also set the historical context. In my novel *Coyote Winds* I inserted

Coyote Winds is a work of fiction. Any resemblance to actual events or persons, living or dead, is entirely coincidental. The Dust Bowl and the Great Depression, however, were very real. For the purpose of the story, I condensed some of the historical events into two years, while in reality the dust storms, food riots, and other historical events played out over several years.

Suppose you've taken a historical figure and given him or her dialogue and personality. Here's how D. M. Thomas dealt with using Freud as a character in *The White Hotel*: *The role played by Freud in this narrative is entirely fictional. My imagined Freud does, however, abide by the generally known facts of the real Freud's life, and I have sometimes quoted from his works and letters, passim. The letters... and all the passages relating to psychoanalysis... have no factual basis.*

The lesson here is if you've taken liberties with historical facts and figures, be open about it. Make your disclaimer part of the experience of the book.

Memoir

Many memoir writers use plain vanilla disclaimers: *This book is memoir. It reflects the author's present recollections of experiences over time. Some names and characteristics have been changed, some events have been compressed, and some dialogue has been recreated.*

That works fine, but some of the great memoir writers use their literary voices to a much better effect.

Mary Karr, in her memoir *The Liars' Club*, apologizes for nothing. She starts the book with her sister asking her mother whether a bullet hole in the kitchen wall happened when her mother shot at her father. No, her mother explains. That's where she shot at Larry. She points at another wall. "Over there's where I shot at your daddy."

As Karr explains, *when fortune hands you such characters, why bother to make stuff up?*

In *This Boy's Life* Tobias Wolff buries his disclaimer in his acknowledgments. As he thanks those who read drafts of the book, he says, *I have been corrected on some points, mostly of chronology. Also my mother claims that a dog I describe as ugly was actually quite handsome. I've allowed some of these points to stand, because this is a book of memory, and memory has its own story to tell. But I have done my best to make it tell a truthful story.*

John Mayberry, a fellow author and attorney, crafted an excellent disclaimer for his memoir, *Waiting for Westmoreland*:

This work depicts actual events in the life of the author as truthfully as recollection permits and/or can be verified by research. Occasionally, dialogue consistent with the character or nature of the person speaking has been supplemented. All persons within are actual individuals; there are no composite characters. The names of some individuals have been changed to respect their privacy.

And Michael N. Marcus wrote the following for his memoir, *Stories I'd Tell My Children (But Maybe Not Until They're Adults)*:

I changed the names of some nice people to maintain their privacy. I changed names of some bad people if I'm no longer as pissed off as I used to be and I don't want to embarrass them or their descendants. Or if I think someone might sue me or beat me up.

Nonfiction

Interestingly, I thumbed through a lot of nonfiction books and found no disclaimers. I suspect the authors and publishers stand on their own research without hiding behind a disclaimer. But I found a great one in Rebecca Skloot's *The Immortal Life of Henrietta Lacks*. Her disclaimer turns the traditional fiction disclaimer on its head: *This is a work of nonfiction. No names have been changed, no characters invented, no events fabricated.*

In contrast, any book giving professional advice, whether it's business, legal, medical, or tax advice, is full of disclaimers. Look at my first chapter.

Here's another excellent disclaimer. I found this one in the program notes for *Roe*, a play by

Lisa Loomer that explores the people and the passions surrounding the *Roe v. Wade* Supreme Court decision. The play uses the names and biographical information of real people in dramatized and fictionalized scenes.

This play is a fictional dramatization based on a true story and real events and was drawn from a variety of sources, including published materials and interviews. For dramatic and narrative purposes, the play contains fictionalized scenes, composite and representative characters and dialogue, and time compression. The views and opinions expressed in the play are those of the characters only and do not necessarily reflect or represent the views and opinions held by individuals on which those characters are based.

Legal Effect of Disclaimers

Legal disclaimers are like chicken soup when you have a cold. They can't hurt and might help. While they are unlikely to stop a lawsuit, they may put an obstacle in the way. Spend a little time on your disclaimer. Use it as an opportunity to explain your purpose and point of view, and most of all, to highlight your literary voice.

CHAPTER ELEVEN

TAX BASICS

THE SAD FACT is that over 40% of every dollar earned goes back to the government in taxes on the federal, state, or local level. Income taxes, employment taxes, and sales taxes take big bites out of your cash flow, not to mention the hours lost to filling out tax forms. Is there any way to reduce the time and money swallowed up by taxes?

If you followed the steps outlined in earlier chapters about obtaining an EIN, Resale Certificate, and business license; using a DBA; and separating your self-publishing finances from your personal finances, then you are well on your way to saving money and managing your taxes efficiently. The payoff comes at tax time.

What follows is a general overview of the U.S. tax issues facing indie authors. The technical details would fill bookshelves, and this chapter alone cannot cover all scenarios. I have touched on areas where the law has been fairly static for a few years, but tax rulings are always evolving.

Income Tax

What Is Income?

Your writing income will include royalties, whether paid by check or via electronic transfers into your bank account, direct sales (such as at book fairs), and speaking fees. If someone lends you money, the loan amount is not income (unless the lender forgives the debt). If someone reimburses you for an expense, the reimbursement is not income, as long as you do not deduct the same expense from income. That's double dipping.

What Is Deductible?

Ordinary and necessary expenses of operating your business are deductible, including

- office supplies and postage,

- costs of writing and research books,

- magazine subscriptions,

- telephone charges,

- printing costs for business cards, bookmarks, and postcards,

- advertising costs,

- costs for software, such as design, video-editing, manuscript editing, and analytics,

- fees and royalties paid for fonts, images, music, and other content,

- writing-club dues,

- website-hosting and online-backup costs,

- subscription costs for HootSuite or other web-based services,

- payments to freelancers, such as editors, copyeditors, designers, web designers, and publicists,

- research expenses, including travel,

- contest entry fees,

- copyright registration fees, and

- a portion of your car and home expenses.

Not surprisingly, determining income and expenses for tax purposes is complicated. In some cases, you may not deduct expenses in the month or year you actually pay them. Here are some examples:

Capital assets. If you purchase a new computer, printer, scanner, or other asset that will be used for more than one tax year, you may have to allocate the cost over several tax years. The technical term is *depreciation*.

Costs of Goods Sold. The expense of buying inventory (including the cost of shipping it to you) is not deductible until you sell, use, or dispose of that inventory. If in one year you buy 500 books from your POD provider and resell 200, give away 100, and toss out 10 because you spilled coffee on them, you may deduct the cost of 310 books. Notice I say cost, which means printing plus shipping costs, not the retail price. The cost of the remaining 190 books is not deductible until you sell, give away, or dispose of the books. For that reason (and for sales tax reasons) it's important to keep track of how many copies of your print book you order and how and when they go out the door.

This is a highly simplified explanation of Costs of Goods Sold. If the bulk of your sales is from your own inventory (and not through online retailers such as Amazon), then work with an accountant to determine if research, editorial, design, and other expenses should be factored into Cost of Goods Sold. The permutations are too varied to be covered here.

Cash basis. Most likely, your accounting will be on a "cash basis" and not an "accrual basis." Explaining the difference would take an accounting course, so take my word for it. You do not count income until you actually receive it. For instance, you may know on November 30, 2018, what royalties are due from Amazon for the month, but if you do not receive those royalties until January 2019, then the royalties will be considered income in 2019, not 2018.

If you work from home, you may be entitled to a home-office deduction. If you use your car for self-publishing activities, you may deduct a portion of your automobile expenses, including lease or loan payments, repairs, gas, and insurance; or you may take a deduction on a per-mile basis. As I mentioned above, use your datebook or calendar to keep track of your work-related miles during the year.

Reporting Payments to Freelancers

If in any calendar year you pay a independent contractor and U.S. taxpayer (other than a corporation) $600 or more for services or $10 or more in royalties in connection with your trade or business, then tax law requires you report those payments on a 1099-MISC and the equivalent state form.

Most likely, you are going to pay an editor, cover designer, website designer, and/or publicist $600 or more. Remember, this does not apply to payments to a corporation such as BookBaby, CreateSpace, or IngramSpark.

If you will cross that payment threshold, ask the freelancer for a W-9. It is a simple form and merely verifies the freelancer's Social Security Number or EIN. You can download the form from the IRS website.

If the independent contractor is a not a U.S. resident, then the rules are different. The law requires you to withhold 30% of your payment to a foreign independent contractor and pay it to the IRS. You can get around this rule by having the independent contractor sign and send you a completed IRS Form 8233. If the independent contractor provides that signed form to you and lives in Canada, South Africa, the European Union, Switzerland, Russia, or a Scandinavian country, then you don't have to withhold any amount. You do not file the Form 8233 with the IRS. You keep it in your files in case the IRS ever asks for verification.

And there's more... .

No later than January 31 of the next calendar year, complete a 1099-MISC for each freelancer, file it with the IRS, and deliver a copy to the freelancer.

You can't download a 1099-MISC because it has multiple, carbon-copy pages. You can get them from a CPA and some office supply stores and post offices. Or order them from the IRS website.

If you report the freelancer's payments on a 1099-MISC, then you are in a better position to deduct the expense from your income. In fact, many CPAs recommend that you send a 1099-MISC to all independent contractors, even if you pay them less than $600 in a calendar year. This provides more support for your business-expense deductions.

Some freelancers may balk at providing a W-9 or having you report their payments on a 1099. Perhaps they are not reporting all their income. But to deduct these expenses without raising red flags with the IRS, you must file and deliver 1099s.

Self-Employment Taxes

If your taxable net income (income less deductible expenses) from writing/publishing is *$400 or more* in any calendar year, you are required to pay self-employment tax equal to approximately 15% of your writing/publishing income. Yes, this is on top of income taxes.

If you are used to getting a paycheck, then your employer pays 50% of your self-employment taxes. However, on income you earn from self-employment, *you pay the employer and the employee portions of Social Security tax and Medicare tax.* You have to pay these self-employment taxes even if your total income is so low that you do not have to pay regular income tax. Ouch!

You calculate the amount of self-employment income at the same time you prepare your 1040, Schedule C, and the rest of your tax forms.

If your taxable income is more than $120,000, then the rules get more complicated. You should work with an accountant once you achieve that income level.

Estimated Taxes

If you are making so much in writing/publishing income that *taxes on that income are $1,000 or more per year*, then congratulations! You do not have to worry about hobby rules, at least during your profitable years. But unfortunately, you are required to pay estimated taxes.

When you work for someone else, your employer withholds a portion of your income to cover your tax obligations. But when you are self-employed, you have to take care of your own withholding by estimating your total tax obligation for the year and making estimated payments to cover that tax obligation. If you don't pay enough in estimated taxes, you could be hit with a penalty equal to 10% of the underpayment.

If you are using a bookkeeping software program, it should calculate your estimated tax payments for you.

Estimated tax payments are due on the following dates:

Income period	Payment due date
January 1 to March 31	April 15
April 1 to May 31	June 15

June 1 to August 31	September 15
September 1 to December 31	January 15 of the following year

These payments used to be called *quarterlies*, but as you see, payment dates no longer coincide with calendar quarters, yet another thing to confuse taxpayers.

Adjust your payments up and down as the year goes on so the total estimated payments stay in line with your total expected tax liability. Be sure to pay the full amount of estimated taxes no later than January 15 of the year following the end of the tax year. (No later than January 15, 2017, for income received in 2016.) Otherwise, you might pay a penalty.

And yes, you probably have to pay estimated taxes to your state as well.

Here's a chart summarizing these tax thresholds:

If you pay an individual	More than $600 in any year	You must get a W-9 from and deliver a 1099-MISC to that individual.
If your taxable income from your self-employed business is	$400 or more in any year	You must pay self-employment tax on that income.
If your taxes on your self-employed income are	$1000 or more in any year	You must pay estimated taxes on that income.

Tax Reporting

At the end of each year, you will report your business income and expenses on a Schedule C, which is then attached to your 1040 Income Tax Return. Your net income or net loss will be added to or subtracted from your other income.

Also prepare a similar tax form with your state.

Preparing your Schedule C is beyond the scope of this *Handbook*. If you use a CPA or tax preparer, your organized bookkeeping will save them time and you money.

If you are preparing your tax returns yourself, there are a number of resources available, including Carol Topp's website and her book *Business Tips and Taxes for Writers* and the most recent Writers Tax Workbook by N. S. Smith and E. M. Linley.

Software is available to help complete your tax returns. But nothing replaces a skilled accountant or enrolled agent. These professionals often identify savings that more than cover their fees.

Sales and Use Taxes

Sales taxes are a major headache for most authors. Some authors say, "Don't worry about it. No one will ever know." However, with computer technology, the chances of getting hit with penalties and interest are increasing.

Below are the basics. The details are enough to drive anyone crazy.

How Much Is the Sales Tax?

It depends on the location of the *buyer*. In California, the tax rate varies by city and county.

You would expect there to be an app that would calculate the sales tax automatically depending on your location. As of now, there are expensive software programs, but no free or inexpensive apps, so you will have to look up the sales tax for each location.

Sales tax is based on the selling price of the item, not on net profit from the sale. If you sell a book at $12, but you bought it from your POD provider for $5, you pay sales tax on the entire $12, not on your profit of $7. You have to pay sales taxes even if your business operates at a loss.

What Sales Are Subject to Sales Tax?

Again, it depends. If you sell print books in person, such as at a reading or book fair, or over the internet to buyers *in your own state*, then by law you are required to pay sales taxes on the print books sold, although you may collect it from buyers.

Twenty-five states are now charging sales tax on digital downloads as well, so sales tax may apply if you are delivering your ebook or other content directly to buyers via downloads if you and the buyers are in a state that imposes a sales tax on digital downloads.

If you are filling internet or telephone orders for a customer in another state, you may also be required to pay sales tax to the buyer's state, but only if you have a business presence (sometimes called a *nexus*) in that state.

What Is a Business Presence?

This is controversial. Some states have enacted legislation that requires large online sellers to collect sales tax even if the seller has no physical presence in the state. These laws are referred to as *Amazon laws* for obvious reasons. The rules are full of technicalities and always changing.

For most writers, you will be considered to have a presence in the state if you have a home there or are selling books at venues in that state, such as a conference or book fair.

The web is littered with misinformation about sales tax. When in doubt, go to the source, such as the sales-tax publications prepared by your state.

Yes, all this is ridiculously confusing, so I tried to summarize the most important guidelines below:

- If you are selling books yourself from your home state to a buyer in your home state, then you pay sales tax at the rate applicable to the location of the sale, or if you are mailing the book, the location of the buyer.

- If you are selling books yourself at a conference or book fair out of state, then you pay sales tax on books that you physically hand over in that state. If you go home and ship books, then the interstate rules apply.

- If you are using PayPal, Square, or a similar service to process your direct sales, add sales tax to the purchase price. You are responsible for reporting and paying the sales tax collected.

- If the bookstore where you do a reading handles the sales to customers, then it is up to the store to collect and pay the sales tax. You don't have to do anything.

- If you are selling through Amazon and online sites other than your own, they will collect and pay the sales tax. You do not have to do anything.

- If you sell your book for a flat amount, let's say $15, write SALES TAX INCLUDED on the receipt. It will be up to you to figure out what portion of the $15 is sales tax. For example, if the applicable sales tax is 8%, then the breakdown for a book sold for $15.00 would be $13.89 for the book and $1.11 for sales tax.

- Many states are applying sales taxes to ebooks and other downloads. Expect this trend to continue. Research the rules for your state.

- Shipping and handling charges are not subject to sales tax if they do not exceed your actual costs.

Go to your local office-supply store and buy a receipt book that makes a carbon copy for each sale. Make a receipt out for customers, and make a receipt for yourself when you give away a book. Keep those receipts.

The flip side is when you buy books from your POD provider, such as CreateSpace, *with the intention of reselling them*, you do not have to pay sales taxes on your purchase as long as you have a Resale Certificate or Seller's Permit, as I discussed earlier. Supply the POD provider with a copy of your Resale Certificate. Sometimes they will accept the certificate number only.

Only items purchased for resale are exempt from sales tax, namely copies of your book. Office supplies (paper, ink, etc.), computers, bookmarks, and business cards are subject to sales tax because you are using them, not reselling them.

If you buy books without paying sales tax on your purchase, and instead give the books away to reviewers and friends or submit them to contests, then you are required to report those giveaways as if they were sales at the wholesale price and pay *use tax* on each book. Use tax is the equivalent to sales tax, but applies to items you use.

You will report your sales (including sales to yourself on books given away) on sales-tax returns filed quarterly or annually depending on the state. In California, you can fill in the forms online. Once you register for a Resale Certificate, the state will hound you for these returns.

There are substantial penalties for failing to file returns (even if you have no sales) and failing to account accurately for sales. You are expected to maintain books and records of all taxable transactions for four years after your annual filing.

Would it be easier to pay the POD provider sales tax on books you buy so you don't have to worry about calculating, collecting, and paying sales tax when you resell the books? No. If you pay the POD provider sales tax that's based on a price of $4 a copy, but then you resell your books for

$12 a copy, you are supposed to collect sales tax on the $8 markup and pay it to the state. I have no idea how many people actually comply with any of these requirements.

Ready to throw your hands up in the air? I don't blame you. But keeping track of sales taxes is not as bad as it sounds. If you keep decent records, then filing the returns will not be too time-consuming.

Tax Basics Checklist

☐ You have developed a system of tracking income and expenses, including retaining all royalty reports and receipts.

☐ You have created a method for counting inventory coming in and heading out the door.

☐ You have obtained W-9s from all U.S. taxpayers to whom you will pay $600 or more in any calendar year.

☐ You are ready to pay self-employment taxes if your writing income is $400 or more per year.

☐ You are ready to pay estimated taxes if taxes on your writing income is $1,000 or more per year.

☐ You have purchased a receipt book to record the amount and location of all sales, including sales to yourself.

CHAPTER TWELVE

MARKETING AND DISTRIBUTION

Getting the Attention You Deserve

AFTER YOU HAVE your manuscript edited and designed, it is time to build your readership. This is a two-step process. First, readers must be aware your book is available and worth reading. Second, you must place the book in their hands either as an ebook or print book.

Since you will not have a traditional publishing company lining up reviews, scheduling interviews, and placing advertisements on your behalf, you will be your own marketing director. If you are working with a self-publishing service company (SPSC), your package may include some marketing services such as promotional copies and prepaid *Kirkus* and *Clarion* reviews. Even with these services, 99% of the marketing work falls on your shoulders.

Your mailbox will be flooded with offers for products or services that will claim to sell thousands of books, launch your book to the top of Amazon's rankings, and let you quit your day job. They will offer to advise you on how to choose keywords and categories, how to create banners, and how to build a platform. Be cautious and skeptical when you read these ads. In marketing, there are no miracles—only hard work and luck. You have to plant a lot of seeds and hope at least one of them grows into a tree.

Again, this *Handbook* focuses on the legal issues of marketing. I'll let others explore the get-rich-quick ideas.

Reviews

Nothing sells books better than five-star reviews. They increase visibility on Amazon's search engine, generate blog posts and interviews, and boost credibility. Good reviews beget more good reviews.

So, it is not surprising that five-star reviews are being manipulated and monetized. No doubt you have heard about sock-puppetry—authors posting reviews, comments, and tweets under fake names. But that is small potatoes. Paid reviews have become a big business. *The New York Times* reported on a site called GettingBooksReviewed.com, which offered 50 positive reviews for $999. The website owner was pulling in $28,000 a month, and the reviewers were not even reading the books. The news story generated so much backlash that the website shut down, and Amazon deleted all the paid-for reviews it could identify.

In fact, Amazon removes many reviews that it decides are "promotional" rather than legitimate. I have never had it happen to me, but I hear from other writers about disappearing reviews. It's quite a blow to lose five-star reviews, but if you want to sell your books through Amazon, you have to play by their rules.

In trying to protect the integrity of the review system, Amazon reserves the right to remove reviews. Here is a portion of their policy as of December 2016.

> *We don't allow anyone to write customer reviews as a form of promotion and if we find evidence that a customer was paid for a review, we'll remove it. If you have a direct or indirect financial interest in a product, or are perceived to have a close personal relationship with its author or artist, we'll likely remove your review. We don't allow authors to submit customer reviews on their own books even when they disclose their identity. When we find unusually high numbers of reviews for a product posted in a short period of time, we may restrict the number of non-Amazon Verified Purchase reviews on that product. If you think we got it wrong and removed a customer review that we shouldn't have, please e-mail us and we will take another look.*

Paid Reviews

Despite Amazon's policy against promotional reviews, they will allow authors to post reviews from certain industry book-review magazines even though the authors paid considerable money.

These magazine reviews are considered legitimate, and you may post excerpts on Amazon, on your website, and in your book, subject to some rules imposed by each site. The quality of the reviews ranges from a high-school book report to a thoughtful essay. The magazines do not guarantee a favorable review, although some will permit you to make an unfavorable review disappear. You have to pay your money and take your chances.

As of December 2016, the larger sites and their prices are as follows:

- *Kirkus Reviews.* For a review of 250–300 words, $425 for standard turnaround of 7 to 9 weeks; $575 for expedited turnaround of 4 to 6 weeks.

- *ForeWord/Clarion Reviews.* For a review of 450 words, $499 for 4- to 6-week turnaround.

- *BlueInk Review.* $395 for 7- to 9-week turnaround; $495 for "Fast Track" 4- to 5-week turnaround.

- Combination of *ForeWord/Clarion* and *BlueInk* Fast Track review, $695.

- *Midwest Book Review.* No fees (unless you are sending an ebook or unpublished manuscript; then the fee is $50). Not all submitted books are reviewed. Long turnaround time, 14 to 16 weeks.

- *YourFirstReview.com.* For a review of 300 words, $149. They estimate a 5- to 7-business-day turnaround for digital books, and 10 or more business days for physical books.

- *PacificBookReview.com.* Various packages include a review of 400–600 words, posting of the review on retail sites, press releases, and additional promotional materials. Prices range from $300 to $495, The turnaround is 5 to 7 weeks for the $300 package, 3 weeks for the $350 and $495 packages.

- *SelfPublishingReview.com.* For a review of 500 words and a 30-day turnaround, packages range from $159 to $299. For a 200-word review, $99 and a 14-day turnaround.

This list is not complete. More sites offering paid reviews are launching every month.

Reviews by Bloggers

Thousands of bloggers will review books if they meet certain criteria. Search for bloggers who cover your genre and have a significant following. Before approaching the blogger, read the blog's review policies. Some will not accept self-published books. Others are particular about what they will read.

The best of these bloggers post their reviews on their blog and also on Amazon, Barnes & Noble.com, and Goodreads, even if they are negative. Unlike *Kirkus* and *ForeWord,* bloggers are unlikely to delete a negative review.

Good publicists and social-media consultants connect you with bloggers. I have seen advertisements for companies that canvass bloggers for you and claim to have a list of bloggers waiting to read and review your book—for a price. These services would save you hours, but I do not know whether they generate any sales.

If you review books on your blog, I recommend you disclose in a "clear and conspicuous manner" whether you received the book for free and whether you will receive a commission on any sale made through your site, such as through an affiliate program. No special lawyer language is needed. Plain English will work.

Unpaid Reviews

Other sources for reviews are your friends, neighbors, family, and fellow writers. I see no problem with giving away free books and asking for a review, as long as you couch the request with, "If you like the book, I'd sure appreciate a review."

Prepare yourself. I find that for every five people who say they will write a review, maybe one comes through. Maybe.

The reviews with the most integrity are those you receive from unknown buyers of your book. Nothing feels sweeter than receiving a glowing review from a stranger. Knowing you touched a reader enough for her to write a five-star review makes all the work and expense of writing and self-publishing worthwhile.

Advertising

It goes without saying that your advertisements must be truthful. Don't claim awards you have not won or make up blurbs from famous writers. Don't laugh; this happens.

Advertising opportunities are so vast, I cannot address them here except to give guidance on what to look for when spending your advertising dollars.

First, before you commit to an advertising buy, try to determine if the channel is effective. Contact authors advertising on the site or publication. Check their sales rankings on Amazon. If the rankings are dismal, take that as a warning. I considered advertising in the Independent Press Listing of the *New York Review of Books*. The prestige of the publication intrigued me. When I scanned the Amazon rankings of the books being advertised, many were down in the depths. I passed.

Advertising rates are highly negotiable. Communicate with the sales staff directly. You are likely to get a substantial discount off the publicized "rack rate." If you are committing significant money, do so only with well-established sites and publications. If the venue goes under, you are unlikely to see your money again.

As always, read your contract. If the salesperson makes promises, make sure those promises are captured in writing.

Email and Newsletters

Email announcements or blasts (known as e-blasts) are the modern version of junk mail. You can purchase mailing lists focused on a particular market—such as middle-school history teachers, personal trainers for seniors, or chinchilla owners—from companies such as ListGIANT. You could build one yourself using your contacts on Twitter, LinkedIn, and other sites.

Try aligning your book with a cause, and ask charitable organizations to promote your book to their members in return for a percentage of sales. With email and direct-mail campaigns, prepare yourself for a low response rate. A 1% to 2% response rate is considered successful.

Email blasts and newsletters are spam, even if you are emailing people who have opted into receiving your material. If you send them using your standard email box, your email address and perhaps your domain may be shut down by your ISP for being a spammer. Use a service such as MailChimp or Constant Contact to send out bulk emails and newsletters. Not only do they provide the opt-out service required with spam, they include helpful analytics.

Distribution of Print Books

Traditionally published books are distributed as follows:

1. The publisher sells the book to a distributor or wholesaler at up to a 70% discount from the suggested retail price.

2. The distributor or wholesaler then sells the book to a retailer at a 40% to 55% discount from the suggested retail price.

3. The retailer then sells the book to readers at whatever price it chooses.

4. If the books don't sell, the retailer sends the books back through the chain and gets a refund.

Suppose the publisher sets the suggested retail price of a book at $15.00. The distributor or wholesaler buys it from the publisher for $4.50, then turns around and sells it to the retailer for $7.50. The retailer puts the book on its shelves at $12.99. If the book doesn't sell, the retailer returns the book to the wholesaler, who then returns it to the publisher, and everyone gets all or most of their money back. The publisher is stuck with boxes of unsold books and sells them cheap to a remainder company.

Discount Rates

Before you launch your book, you will need to select a discount rate at which your book will be sold to wholesalers. Many SPSCs and POD companies permit authors to set their own discount rate at something between 20 and 70%. Some encourage you to set a high discount so bookstores will order copies; others do the opposite and urge a low discount rate to increase your earnings.

You must also decide whether you will accept returns of unsold books. Some SPSCs accept returns for you, but they charge a high price for the service whether or not your books are ever distributed to bookstores, and whether or not you ever have any returns. CreateSpace will not accept returns, but IngramSpark and Lightning Source will. You may opt to have returns shipped to you or destroyed.

All this is great in theory, but the truth is that no matter how much you discount your book, you are unlikely to get any shelf space at a brick-and-mortar store. Retailers are unlikely to sacrifice valuable space to an unknown author. The big publishers have sales teams to promote their books and offer incentives ($$) to have their books featured in windows and on table displays. Plus, they offer a range of titles you'll never match. For most self-published authors, hiring a sales team is not in the budget.

When SPSCs and POD providers purport to provide "distribution to major retailers," it means your book will be listed in the catalogues of Ingram, Baker & Taylor, and other wholesalers. That's it. Distribution does not mean your book will appear in stores, only that the stores may order it.

Self-publishing experts recommend you set your discount rate as low as possible (let's say 40% off the retail price) and focus your efforts on selling your print books through internet channels such as Amazon, B&N's online store, and other online sellers. Your book will still be available to brick-and-mortar stores, but expect any sales to be special orders by customers.

Once your books are selling well, then increase your discount rate so that is in line with traditionally published books.

If you are using offset printing, high discounts are less of a problem because your costs could be cut in half. You could store and ship the books yourself or engage a fulfillment company to store and ship for you. If you are publishing a fine-arts book or are expecting to sell a relatively high volume of books, offset is a viable option. But none of this solves the problem of convincing bookstores to buy your book, other than on consignment.

Consignment Agreements

Many independent bookstores will host readings and carry books published by local authors. Instead of buying the books from Ingram or other suppliers, local bookstores get the books directly from you on consignment, which means you continue to own the books. The store does not buy them from you, but agrees to try to sell them for you. If they sell the book, they keep a percentage (typically 40 to 50%), and the rest goes to you. (They handle sales tax.)

No need to confine yourself to the local bookstore. Contact stores where you grew up, where you vacation, and where you have set your story. *Coyote Winds* is set in eastern Colorado and was sold on consignment at Tattered Cover bookstores in Denver.

Don't be surprised and don't object if the store disclaims any responsibility for theft, damage, or lost books. Also, many stores charge a marketing or setup fee ranging from $25 to $75. While this is an unfair burden on the self-published author, most independent bookstores operate on thin profit margins. If you cannot afford the fee, ask the store if they will waive it.

Consignment agreements usually expire after 90 days, but in my experience, the stores keep the books on their shelves for a lot longer.

KDP Select

KDP Select is an optional program offered through Amazon. If you sign up for the program, you agree to sell your ebook exclusively through Amazon's Kindle for a period of 90 days and to suspend sales through all other digital channels, including Smashwords, iBookstore, and your own website. This does not affect print and audio books; you may continue to distribute them through any channels.

In return, you may choose between two promotional tools: Kindle Countdown Deals (limited-time promotional discounting) or Free Book Promotions (free downloads for up to 5 days in every 90-day period).

Kindle Countdown Deals and Free Book Promotions are so popular there are thousands of discounted and free ebooks offered every day. Online, you'll find plenty of advice on how to manage and promote your Kindle promotional days. They get the books into the hands of more readers. Since nothing sells books better than word-of-mouth, these readers will hopefully become more mouths to spread the word.

If your ebook is enrolled in KDP Select, it will be available for lending to Amazon Prime members and for downloading through the Kindle Unlimited Program. You will receive a share of revenues from those programs based on the number of pages read. The payments from KDP Select are very low, so consider this program as a short-term way to promote your book, not as a long-term moneymaker.

Marketing and Distribution Checklist

In this chapter, we have explored methods for promoting your book, including

- ☐ obtaining reviews,

- ☐ sending out mass emails and newsletters,

- ☐ selecting advertising channels,

- ☐ being realistic about your book appearing on bookstore shelves,

- ☐ setting discount rates, and

- ☐ entering into consignment agreements with bookstores.

CHAPTER THIRTEEN

AVOIDING SCAMS AND MYTHS

RECENTLY, I RECEIVED an email from someone trying to help her 92-year-old father. Her father had published a memoir through a large SPSC. The SPSC had talked him into various marketing and "Hollywood" packages costing over $30,000. Yes, that's right. $30,000—not $3,000.

They would call him late in the day, a time most elderly people living alone are particularly vulnerable. They would stay on the phone with him for an hour, asking about his life, his children, his grandchildren, his dogs. They would say they loved his memoir. They would talk about legacy and leaving something for future generations. They'd offered him "special, you-only, today-only" deals. Once, when he said no, the salesperson begged him to buy the package, saying she would get fired if she didn't make the sale after spending so much time talking with him. He bought the package.

Stories like this make me furious. And sadly, they are far too common.

Wherever money is to be made, scammers are scheming to take it from you. They promise legacy, income, exposure, and freedom from your day job. They brag about off-the-chart successes. Their websites are often fabulous and tempting.

If your books are not selling well, you will be tempted to listen to them. Authors are particularly vulnerable since anyone who writes a book tends to be a dreamer. We hope to find the secret formula to success. Perhaps for $99, or $199, or $999, we will be admitted into that exclusive club.

In all fairness, not all of these offers are scams; some of these companies are selling *myths*.

They deliver the listing, the blog tour, the tweets, or other service they promise, but the boost in sales never happens. Myths are a waste of money, just like scams.

If you are under 25 or over 65, you are the prime target for scammers and aggressive salespeople. Younger writers may not have the experience to recognize a con or a pressured sale, and older writers tend not to ask questions for fear of appearing out-of-touch, out-of-date, or simply slow or cranky. Older victims tend not to tell anyone they have been scammed, fearing their families will take away their car, their cash, their freedom, and stick them in a home.

Scammers and aggressive salespeople know all this and take advantage of it. They prey on your wish to be someone special and to be remembered.

Be careful. When someone is asking you to part with your money, don't let them intimidate, entice, or guilt you into buying a service you do not need or paying above-market prices. You have the right to ask as many questions as you want. You have the right to say no. You have the right to hang up on them. Go ahead. You'll enjoy the feeling of control.

Common Come-Ons

Some common offers for separating you from your cash:

Companies that charge for services that are virtually free. For example, U.S. copyright registration costs $35 plus two copies of your book and takes about ten minutes. I cannot see paying someone $150 or $200 for the service. Or setting up a Goodreads giveaway, also free. I would not pay good money to someone to upload my manuscript to CreateSpace or KDP, or to set up a Twitter, Pinterest, or other social media site for me, something I could also do myself for free in less time than it would take to give these goons my credit card number. If the technology intimidates you, then ask a family member or friend to help you. Trust me; none of these tasks are difficult.

Algorithm busters. Before long, you will receive offers for software and services to enhance your searchability on Amazon, Google, and other sites. There are companies that claim to have cracked Google's and Amazon's algorithms, but much of their advice is speculation and is available for free on various blogs. And the algorithms are constantly changing, so what you buy today may be worthless next week. There's no need to cough up $49 or $99 or $199 for this service.

Book fair packages. Some companies offer you a chance to appear and sign books at their tables at prestigious book fairs. The price? A mere $1,000 and up. You might be "invited" from a select group. Before you jump at the opportunity, look into the book fair. Chances are, if you team up with a few other authors, you could get your own table at the fair at a fraction of the price.

Literary agents or publishers who charge reading fees. Any legitimate literary agent or publisher will *not* charge a reading fee. Avoid any agent or publisher who charges to read, review, prescreen, or evaluate your work.

SPSCs and vanity presses that mislead. Some SPSCs are, or border on being, scams. I am not talking about charging exorbitant fees or requiring authors to purchase hundreds, if not thousands, of copies of their books. Those are bad enough. However, if an SPSC promises services that it does not deliver, performs substandard work (including delays), charges hidden fees, claims exclusive or perpetual rights to the author's work, or fails to report and pay royalties honestly, then that SPSC is a *scammer,* if not worse. I include in that category any SPSC or vanity publisher that pretends to be selective about the projects it accepts, as if it were a traditional press. Such companies convince unsuspecting writers that they have achieved an honor, and the prize is to part with their hard-earned money and sometimes their copyright. Also, in the scamming bucket go the SPSCs that force writers to buy thousands of copies of their own books, typically at high prices.

So-called religious presses. Most religious SPSCs and presses are legitimate. But I have seen websites for companies that call themselves Christian. The sites are laced with comfort words like *values, trust,* and *community,* yet have the most egregious and overreaching contracts, including appropriating people's copyrights. This is the lowest form of scam—hiding behind a religious façade.

Getting on the list. There's nothing hotter than being on the right list. I'm not talking about bestseller lists here, but lists that claim to give you a competitive edge in the industry. For example, for $50 or $250 or $3,500, some companies promise to get you on the list of hot book-group recommendations, popular school visitors, compelling public speakers, or new and noteworthy releases. Some of these lists are miles long. So much for selectivity.

Radio and media packages. Do not be surprised to get a call or email from a purported radio program or media company eager to interview you. They promise to feature your interview in hundreds of media outlets, because they *love* your work. There's a catch. To get any more than the basic internet interview, you will need to cough up a media promotion fee of up to $5,000.

Bogus industry review sites. Some sites pretend to be legitimate, unbiased sites that assist you in choosing the right SPSC for your book. But look at the site carefully, especially the fine print at the bottom. The site could be operated by an SPSC. For instance, chooseyourpublisher.com, e-bookspublishing.com, and poetry-publishers.com are all owned by Author Solutions, a large SPSC that has been sued for misleading marketing practices and breach of contract.

Contests

There are many prestigious and legitimate contests. Some are genre specific, such as the Bram Stoker Award for horror, the Prometheus Award for science fiction, and the Scott O'Dell Award for children's historical fiction. Some are open to self-published works; others are not. Some are vague. If they don't prohibit indie books, jump in and give them a try.

However, some contests charge high entry fees, and whenever there is money involved, there are sharks. Contests are big moneymakers. With entry fees ranging as high as $150, a contest with 2,000 entrants earns $300,000.

Your inbox will be flooded with invitations to enter contests. The sponsors run full-color ads in writers' magazines. They also advertise on Craigslist.

How can you tell the difference between a legitimate contest and the questionable? Ask the following questions:

Who is the sponsor? Is the sponsor a live person or a publication? If the sponsor is a "media" company, such as J. M. Northern Media (which seems to do nothing but sponsor writing contests with sizeable entry fees), you will gain no prestige by winning. Search the contest on Goodreads, Library Thing, or other writers' communities online. If there's no mention of the contest winners, that's a good indication that the contest lacks prestige. Check out the contest's reputation on writing forums such as Absolute Write Water Cooler, Predators and Editors, and Writers Beware.

How high are the fees? Anything over $30 is suspect. If the sponsor is a reputable literary journal or a legitimate writer's conference, a higher fee is acceptable. Those organizations are often starved for cash.

Who are the judges? You would be surprised how many contests do not disclose the names of the judges. They use vague terms like "industry experts." Some contests are "judged" by reader voting, a recipe for cheating.

How many categories are there? The more categories, the more likely the contest is merely a moneymaker.

Do they offer you anything for your money? Some contests offer written critiques or reviews for anyone who places, which may make the entry fee worthwhile.

What are the prizes? A roll of stickers? A certificate printed on someone's inkjet? An invitation to attend a book "festival" at your own expense? Can you find online photos of this supposed festival?

What rights are you giving away? Read the fine print, particularly regarding what commitments you are making. I have seen online contests that ask you to post the first 5,000 words of your book. The small print says you are granting the contest sponsor the right to use those words any way it pleases, even in advertising, without your consent or knowledge.

Are they offering a book contract? If the contest offers publication as a prize and you win, are you granting the sponsor first publishing rights? If so, who will be the publisher? Is it a legitimate press with a catalogue of books? Or is it a self-publishing service company or a vanity press? Are you committed to use that publisher if you win, or can you take a cash prize instead? You would hate to have committed your book to one of these contest sponsors if a traditional publisher comes knocking at your door.

General Guidelines

☐ Don't let ego affect judgment. Flattery softens resolve. If a vendor is overly flattering, give your wallet to someone for safekeeping, particularly someone cynical.

☐ If anything seems too good to be true, it is too good to be true.

☐ Be skeptical of companies that justify higher prices by promising more than their competitors. If they are that good, they would be too busy to be chasing indie authors.

☐ Beware of braggarts. They could turn out to be all talk and no action.

☐ Read testimonials. Are they from the same three people? One person (the owner)? Search those names. Do these people exist? Have they sold a lot of books?

☐ Does the company have a physical address and phone number? Is it a UPS store or other mailbox rental site?

☐ Are you being pressured to decide immediately? If the sales pitch is a one-time offer good for today only, call their bluff. Or better yet, walk way. This sales technique is called "hot boxing" and is an unfair business practice.

☐ See what comes up when you do an online search of the company name plus words like *scam*, or *complaints*, or *sucks*. What you find may be eye opening.

☐ Find out how long the company has been in business. Did they used to operate under another name? Search that name and the name of any people involved with the company. If you see a long string of company names, that is a bad sign.

☐ Search websites such as Predators and Editors, Absolute Write Water Cooler, and Writers Beware. They perform a tremendous service by outing disreputable companies and warning writers.

☐ Develop a good sense of humor. Laugh off these scams. You know better.

CHAPTER FOURTEEN

ESTATE PLANNING FOR WRITERS

IF YOUR BOOKS are successful, your characters may live forever alongside Anna Karenina, David Copperfield, and Frankenstein.

The copyright in your books also lives on. As I explained in Chapter Two, a copyright lasts for the creator's lifetime plus 70 years. So if you publish a book in 2018 and live another 40 years, the copyright will last until 2128. That's 110 years!

Something to think about. And plan for.

Writers should take some time to consider how their intellectual and digital assets will be managed following their death. With a little planning and clear direction, your work is more likely to remain published and income producing. Without planning, you could leave such a mess, no one will want to touch your work.

Self-publishing writers need to pay particular attention to these matters. Since most of us don't have business managers and agents following our careers, the task falls on us to take care of business.

Why We Procrastinate

The news is full of stories of artists dying without wills and leaving behind ugly battles. Prince died earlier this year, and no one has found a will. He left behind one full sister, a number of half-siblings, and several people who claim to be illegitimate children, all clambering for a piece of his estate. I suspect the estate's legal fees will run into the millions of dollars, money Prince would have wanted to go to better and more charitable purposes, no doubt.

Let's confess that no likes estate planning. We avoid estate planning because it involves death. Plus, we fear making the wrong decisions and not being around to correct them mid-course. Whom do we want to leave in charge? Whom can we trust to preserve our legacy and not stick it in a cardboard box, deep in the garage, where the rats nest?

So add estate planning to your to-do list (near the top, please). Here are some basics to help you get started.

How Do Assets Transfer?

Generally, there are four ways assets transfer to heirs.

Intestate. If someone dies without a will or living trust, then the heirs are determined by law. Usually, the assets go to descendants, or if there are no descendants, then to siblings, parents, cousins, etc. If a writer dies intestate, then all the heirs hold the copyright together. Any one of them may publish and exploit the work as books, films, TV, etc., without the permission of the others, although income must be shared. Yes, they could all put out competing editions of your book.

Probate. If someone executes a Will, the Will directs how assets will be distributed. The estate is handled by an Executor named in the Will with supervision by the probate courts.

Living Trust. Using a living trust, a person transfers assets into a trust before death and names himself or herself as the Trustee with power to manage and sell the assets. Upon the death or incapacity of the Trustee, a Successor Trustee automatically takes over those powers. In most cases, the Successor Trustee may distribute the assets without going through the probate court, so the process is simpler and less expensive.

Entity. Some people transfer their assets to a corporation or LLC that will survive their death. This is a more sophisticated structure, and you should engage a trusts-and-estates attorney to determine if this makes sense for you.

Copyright, Property With a Twist

The copyright interest in your work, whether published or unpublished, is a property right that passes to your heirs. Plus, there is an interesting twist to copyright ownership. Under current law, any grant of rights, whether an assignment or license, may be terminable after 35 years. This provision was intended to benefit artists who, for a few dollars, sold creations that went on to be worth millions. If you have licensed your work and it becomes wildly popular after your death, your estate may want to terminate licenses and re-license the work for higher income.

All this means that someone will need to make a lot of decisions after you are gone, including

- whether to continue to publish your work independently or with a traditional publisher,

- when to update your work due to changes in the market or technology,

- how to deal with unpublished work,

- whether to explore other opportunities, such as film and merchandizing,

- whether to create derivative products and prequels/sequels,

- whether to exercise the terminate right with respect to old licenses, and

- when to pursue and sue infringers.

Designating a Literary Trustee

Most experts advise that writers designate someone as a Literary Trustee (LT) in a Will or Living Trust. Your LT may be the same person as your Executor or Successor Trustee, but not necessarily. The LT might be one of your heirs or an independent person, such as an agent, attorney, accountant, or fellow writer. Preferably, your LT will have experience in publishing as well as reliable business and personal judgment.

Generally, I recommend choosing one person as the LT, even if many people will be receiving income from your writings. I have seen too many families get into nasty battles when decision making is shared. Some want instant income, and others want to spread income over time. Old grudges resurface. So the LT should be someone capable of handling these situations.

Spell out the powers of the LT, such as the authority to sign contracts, engage editors and designers, publish and sell books, and collect and distribute royalties to your heirs. You may also give specific instructions, such as directing that certain work not be published until a later date or burned.

Consider giving the LT control of your images, bio, drafts, journals, correspondence, research, and other materials that may be of interest to biographers, libraries, and literary organizations.

Finally, you may want the LT to manage digital assets, such as your blog and social media accounts.

You should find some way to compensate the LT. Otherwise, no one will want to spend the time. Typically, the LT receives a percentage of income generated by the literary assets, with a minimum payment made from your estate up-front.

Finally, be sure to name at least one alternative or successor LT in case your first choice cannot fill the role.

Organizing Your Assets

I'll be blunt about this. Leaving disorganized and incomplete personal and business records is downright cruel to your heirs. Not only are they grieving your loss, they can't figure out whether you cashed your last royalty check. So spend some time getting your documents in order.

- Create a list of your published work, including dates published.

- Create a file with all publishing and related agreements.

- Compile a list of your unpublished work, including where to find that work.

- Register the copyright of your work, especially published work. Registering the copyright creates a permanent record of what your work looked like on the date of registration and makes it easier to transfer to your heirs.

- Update your income and expense records, particularly to show how much you have invested in each book for editing, design, production, and promotional expenses.

- Make a list of user names and passwords and keep it up to date. Include your accounts with CreateSpace, IngramSpark, Smashwords, Draft2Digital, Bookbaby, and other providers involved in the production and distribution of your work. Also include all professional groups such as Authors Guild, Independent Book Publishers Association, Alliance of Independent Authors, etc. For some social media sites and email accounts, you can designate up-front a "legacy" contact who has the right to post to your account or who will be notified if your account is inactive for a long period of time.

- List user names and passwords to your website and email accounts. Email can be used to verify password resets and may contain a useful history of your business dealings.

- Make sure someone knows when to renew your domain registrations. If your registration expires, someone may buy it and charge your heirs a fortune to get it back. Or they might auction it off. This is especially important if your website generates income or referrals.

Hiring an Expert

When you're ready to tackle this project, you can find forms of wills and living trusts online or in books, such as those from NOLO Press.

But no book, form, or blog post can substitute for the advice of an experienced professional. Hire a trusts-and-estates attorney, preferably one with some experience with intellectual property assets. The greater the value of your estate, the more critical it is to have a well-thought-out estate plan. With professional advice, you are more likely to save on taxes, reduce the risk of litigation, and rest assured that your work and your bounty end up where you want them.

And your characters will live on.

Estate Planning Checklist

- ☐ Designate a literary trustee.

- ☐ Create an inventory of your literary assets, both published and unpublished.

- ☐ List user names and passwords for all companies handling the printing and distribution of your work, all writing-related memberships, and all social media accounts.

- ☐ Prepare a will or living trust that meets the legal requirements of your state. You may want to engage an attorney for this step.

CHAPTER FIFTEEN

COLLABORATIONS

WOULDN'T IT BE fun to write a book with your best friend? Or better yet, a writer who's inspired about plots so you can focus on character, or vice versa?

When collaborations work, writing partners complement and support one another. But when they fail, the drama may be as ugly as a Hollywood divorce. For every successful writing partnership, there are dozens of failed ones despite the best of intentions. Not everyone is a team player, and not every team is a winner.

The best way to improve the odds of a successful writing partnership is to *take the time to put the collaboration agreement in writing up-front.*

Most people resist this idea. Like a prenuptial agreement, it kills the romance.

But the process of preparing an agreement may be more valuable than the result. If writers discuss issues at the start, they are less likely to have misunderstandings later. Or you may discover you can't work together. The sooner you realize that, the better.

Before you jump into a co-writing project, write out the following details:

Describe the Project. Fiction, nonfiction, memoir? Even better, create an outline.

Identify personal goals. Successful partners share common goals. If one partner's objective is to cash in with a genre piece and the other dreams of creating timeless literature, expect friction.

Discuss the writing process. Will one partner write the story in narrative form and the other flesh out scenes? Will you draft chapters and trade them for comments? How often will you meet?

Establish ground rules for critiques. Some partners handle bluntness and sarcasm with ease, but most of us prefer a gentler touch. The longer you work together, the easier it gets to give and take criticism. Consider your partner's comments as a gift; she cares enough to help make the work better.

Do a dry run. Work on a shorter piece together, such as a short story or blog post. You'll learn a lot about working mechanics and styles.

Set realistic deadlines. Expect the project to take at least twice as long as planned.

Decide on credits. Will both names appear on the work and in what order? Will credits be listed as A and B, A with B, or A as told to B? Will you use a pen name?

Specify ownership. Unless you agree otherwise, all partners own equal shares in jointly created work. Plus, each partner has the power to sell or license the work without the other partner's consent (although income must be shared). Put your ownership percentages *in writing*. Agree that no partner may sell, license, or transfer any interest in the project without the consent of the other partner. Register the copyright under all names, or the pen name, or all of the above.

Allocate income. I recommend that the partner who had the original idea should own the majority interest, even if it is a token amount (51-49% split). That little bit saves resentment later. However, if one partner handles readings and conferences, that partner should keep a larger portion of sales made at the events.

Deal with expenses. If one partner pays for research, editing, design, and marketing, does that partner recoup expenses before income is shared? If income never covers expenses, does the other partner kick in a share?

Assign non-writing tasks. Who will engage editors, negotiate contracts, handle interviews, and manage social media? Don't take the shortcut of saying responsibilities will be shared equally. It never happens. People gravitate to the tasks they do better, and unpleasant work will be left undone.

Plan for conflict. You will have disagreements. View them as a sign that something is not working in the manuscript. Let go of your ego, and look at the problem a new way, your partner's way. If you cannot agree, decide up-front who gets the final say. If the project was one partner's idea, typically that partner decides. Or pick a third party who is trusted by both sides.

No door slamming. Agree that neither of you will quit without giving the other party notice of what's not working and a chance to fix it. Respect requests for cooling-off periods.

Address legal responsibilities. Each partner should promise that all work contributed will be original, will not be defamatory or infringing, and will not invade privacy or other rights. Don't be foolish about this. If your partner introduces material that is suspect, rewrite or reject it. No matter what your agreement says, both of you may be responsible to third parties.

Face death and disability. What if one of you gets hit by the proverbial bus? Does the other have the right to finish the project with an equitable adjustment in ownership and income? Does all decision-making authority transfer to the surviving partner, or will the heirs or representatives of the deceased or disabled partner have a say?

Deal with termination. If the partnership ends, who owns the work? Who has the right to complete the project? There are no right answers here. The partners need to talk this out.

Let the little stuff slide. Entering into a collaboration means giving up some control. Your partner may have a different approach to a scene, character, or problem. Consider that a good thing. This is why you are working as a team. Laugh together, especially when everything is going wrong.

Reward yourselves. When you finish each chapter, share a bottle of champagne. When you complete the first draft, take yourselves out to dinner.

Keep communicating. If you are feeling unfairly burdened, take the chance of bringing it up— the sooner, the better. Years ago, a friend told me the motto of a happy marriage: "I can't read your f**king mind!" The same is true in writing collaborations.

CHAPTER SIXTEEN

BUSINESS BEYOND THE BOOK

ALTHOUGH PUBLISHING YOUR work has never been easier, making a living as a writer has never been tougher. It's a crowded market, and readers are more and more accustomed to getting content for free. So let's take a look at income opportunities beyond the printed book.

Audio Books

The audio-book market is growing faster than any other format. People are listening to books while they drive, exercise, or simply relax. Listeners don't have to stop when they switch devices, since Kindle's Whispersync enables them to move between audio and ebooks without losing their place.

By far, the most popular digital platform for producing and distributing audio books is Amazon's ACX (Audio Book Creation Exchange). ACX serves two functions. First, it is a matchmaker for authors and narrators (which ACX calls *producers*). Second, it uses Audible to distribute the audio books through Amazon and iTunes, the two biggest retailers of audio books.

Authors post their books on ACX, and producers upload auditions. The author chooses a producer from the auditions, and the author and producer work together to create a final version of the audio book and upload it. Alternatively, authors can narrate their own books and upload them into the ACX system.

In either case, Audible distributes the audio book through Amazon and iTunes. And Audible has the right to distribute the audio book for seven years.

In working with ACX, the author must make two decisions:

- First, the author decides whether to (1) pay the producer an up-front fee for the work (typically between $100 and $1,000 per finished hour) but no royalty on sales, or to (2) split the author's share of audio book royalties 50-50 with the producer and pay no up-front fee.

- Second, the author must decide whether to sell the audio book through Audible on an exclusive or non-exclusive basis.

If the author grants exclusive rights, then the author receives 40% of the retail sales. However, the author agrees not to distribute the audio book through any other channels, including the author's own website. An exclusive agreement with ACX does not affect the author's right to sell the print and ebook versions of the same work.

If the author grants non-exclusive rights, then the royalty rate is 25%. In addition, the author does not have the option to split royalties with the producer and must pay the producer a flat fee. The author retains the right to distribute the audio book through other channels and in other audio formats. Some other distribution options are described below, and others are sure to pop up over time.

Keep in mind that Audible has close to a monopoly on the market. Most likely, the bulk of your audio book sales will be through Audible, so authors may be better off with the exclusive option.

Before you sign up with ACX, there are some drawbacks you should consider.

First, Audible controls pricing. Under KDP and CreateSpace, authors set their own suggested retail price (SRP) and earn royalties based on that SRP. Audible, however, sets the price for the audio books, and royalties are based on actual sales. Audible discounts audio books substantially and offers low subscription pricing. For indie authors accustomed to controlling their pricing, this is hard to accept.

Second, the royalty-splitting option may not get you the best producers. Many of the better producers won't participate in a royalty-sharing agreement unless the book is a top seller. They prefer to be paid a flat rate, typically thousands of dollars. This up-front payment may not be feasible for most authors.

Other Audio Options

Podium Publishing is an interesting option. Podium produces and publishes high-quality audio books and boasts an impressive portfolio (including indie author Andy Weir, author of *The*

Martian). They focus on sci-fi and fantasy. While the Podium contact page says they love to hear from authors, agents, publishers, and listeners, they do not accept submissions. If you have a book that is selling well, it's worth an email to let them know you are interested.

Various companies offer to produce audio books for you. An online search of "audio book producers" will generate dozens of choices. They hire the narrators (with the author's input and approval), produce, and edit the audio book. Some work on a flat fee basis, other on a royalty-sharing basis, and many will negotiate a blended deal.

If you work with any of these companies, make sure you end up with all rights to the finished audio book and you also understand how to terminate the relationship in case the arrangement does not work out.

Some SPSCs say they produce audio books. Frankly, that doesn't appeal to me. They are not experts at producing audio books, so they probably send the project out to other providers. The author ends up with more people with their fingers in the author's cookie jar.

Once you have a completed audio book in hand, and assuming you have decided not to give ACX an exclusive distribution deal, then there are various distribution sites to help get your book into listeners' hands.

Author's Republic is one. This audio-book distribution portal can get an author's work on every major audio-book platform through just one submission, including Audible/iTunes/ Amazon, Audiobooks.com, Barnes & Noble, Scribd, Downpour, OverDrive, and Hoopla. Authors control the price of their audio books and receive a royalty of between 25 and 35% of the retail price, depending on the sales channel.

Finally, authors should also consider selling their audio books as downloads from their own websites. Selling the audio books themselves, authors enjoy the highest royalty rate—100%!

Selling Rights Internationally

Not long ago, selling book rights internationally required a network of agents, publishers, translators, and distributors. It was almost impossible for independent authors to break into the market. But Amazon, social media, email, online retail platforms, and advances in technology have made exploiting international rights easier than ever. Writers can engage with readers all over the world without leaving their desks.

If your book is sold through Amazon, then you are already reaching at least 14 international markets through Amazon's country-specific pages. Many authors spend time and money to set up specialized Amazon Author Pages for each Amazon market. These markets include the United Kingdom, Ireland, Canada, Germany, Italy, Spain, Brazil, Japan, China, India, Mexico, and Australia.

If you are hoping to line up a foreign-based publisher, for your work in either English or translation, considering listing your work on the new online rights global marketing/match-making sites such as IPR License and PubMatch.com. These are subscription-based services costing a few hundred dollars per year. You post your work on a database that is searchable by foreign publishers looking for works to license.

Translations

Many writers engage translators themselves and publish their translated works through CreateSpace and IngramSpark. Three companies that specialize in providing translations are ComTranslations, Harcz & Partner, and Literary Translations. You can also find freelance translators through any of the freelance matchmaking websites such as Upwork.com and Freelancer.com.

Translation requires an up-front investment, typically between $2,500 and $7,000, and often you will be paying the translator a percentage of royalties. Finding a good translator is challenging because capturing the voice and meaning of your work is more art than mechanics. The more literary the writing, the trickier it gets.

Be aware that in some European countries the copyright of the translated work lies with the translator, even if paid an up-front lump sum, unless otherwise specified in a legal agreement.

Not surprisingly, new companies are offering indie authors translation and international marketing services as a bundle. Below are summaries of what Babelcube and Fiberead offer. I expect other companies will be entering this huge market.

Babelcube

Babelcube connects authors with translators and distributes the translated books internationally.

Babelcube's process is similar to ACX's royalty-share structure. The author pays nothing up-front for the translation, but shares royalties with the translator and with Babelcube on a sliding scale depending on the total net revenues generated by the translated book. Basically, the more books sold, the more the author earns.

As of December 2016, the basic terms were as follows:

- For the first $2,000 in net receipts, the author gets 30%, the translator 55%, and Babelcube 15%.

- For net receipts between $2,001 and $5,000, the author gets 45%, the translator 40%, and Babelcube 15%.

- For net receipts between $5,001 and $8,000, the author gets 65%, the translator 20%, and Babelcube 15%.

- For net receipts over $8,000, the author gets 75%, the translator 10%, and Babelcube 15%.

Net receipts means the monetary amount (in U.S. dollars) received by Babelcube from sales of each unit sold by Babelcube and Babelcube's sub-distributors, less any cash incentives, promotional discounts, sales or use taxes, excise taxes, value-added taxes, duties, distribution fees, and returns.

Similar to the process with ACX, the author posts information about the book on the Babelcube site, and potential translators contact the author if they are interested. The author selects the translator and reviews and approves the translation. Once the translation is complete, Babelcube has the exclusive right to distribute the translated version of the book for five years, renewing automatically for one-year periods unless either party gives the other written notice of termination at least 60 days prior to the renewal date. It distributes ebooks through various channels including Amazon, Google, Apple, Nook, Kobo, Scribd, and hundreds of regional and country online retailers and print books through CreateSpace.

The author retains all rights in both the original text and the translated text. The translator assigns to the author all rights to the translation, including copyright and moral rights. The author must provide a cover for the translated work. Babelcube does not offer to sell the author or translator copies of the book at a discount. They must pay to buy the book on Amazon or elsewhere just like any other buyer.

As of December 2016, Babelcube translates works into Afrikaans, Dutch, English, French, German, Italian, Japanese, Norwegian, Portuguese, and Spanish.

Fiberead

Fiberead offers translating and marketing services for the Chinese market. As of December 2016, they translate into simplified and traditional Chinese only.

China represents a huge market. Who wouldn't want to jump in? However, writers should be aware that Fiberead's contract is not author friendly, especially compared to Babelcube's. Among other things,

- Fiberead controls the choice of translators, pricing, and marketing;

- Fiberead retains all rights to the translated work even after the agreement terminates;

- author's royalties are 30% to 40% of net sales receipts for ebooks, but Fiberead deducts all kinds of expenses from the net sales receipts, including publishing fees and marketing costs; and

- Fiberead claims an 18-month exclusive on the print version of the translated book and a right of first offer after that.

Marketing Your Expertise

The process of writing and publishing a book has made you an expert. Perhaps researching your historical novel made you an expert on 12th century weaponry. Or your nonfiction book solidified your knowledge about nourishing children during chemotherapy. Here are some ways to leverage that expertise into more income.

- Solicit speaking engagements. Many pay, plus they increase book sales.

- Run your own conferences, courses, podcasts, YouTube channel, and webinars.

- Set up a paid membership/subscription service for your content.

- Combine efforts with other experts to create joint works.

- Hire yourself out as a coach, consultant, editor, or freelance writer.

- Use your writing to generate business for your day job. Consider your book a business card people don't throw away.

Develop a Business Mindset

I have seen this happen with a lot of writers. Otherwise capable, successful, competent people turn into self-doubting wimps when it comes to pursuing their writing careers. We become embarrassed, even sheepish. Why?

Do we feel guilty? Are we being self-indulgent by taking time away from our jobs and family to write, publish, and promote?

Do we feel silly? Are friends calling us "writers" while making air quotes with their fingertips?

Are we fatalistic? While our culture admires dreamers who pursue Don Quixote quests, it also considers them tragic, predictably so. How many well-meaning heroes die before the end of a movie or novel? Eighty %? Ninety %? Does cynicism justify giving up on dreams? Is there a hidden message here?

Do we feel out of step? Our culture measures a person by what he can buy, not by what he can produce. We glorify those who make their millions fast and easy. No matter how much you reject materialism, does part of you wonder if you are wasting resources that would be better applied to a "real" job? After all, there are faster, easier ways to make money than crafting a novel word by word by word.

Hogwash. In 30 years of practicing business law, I've seen a lot of people succeed and fail. No matter what the business, the number one indicator of success is not intelligence, talent, luck, money, education, connections, ethics, or even lack of ethics, although all of those help.

It's Tenacity—on Steroids.

Successful entrepreneurs have a drive that pushes them on despite obstacles, detours, doubts, debts, and mistakes. (Believe me, they make plenty of mistakes.) They believe that achieving a goal is worth pushing themselves and others to do beyond their best—and breaking some of the "rules" that hold others back.

If Bill Gates or Steve Jobs or Oprah Winfrey were independently publishing, what would they do (riches aside)? They would push, demand, question, negotiate, and micro-manage until they produced the best books possible. They know the road to success requires taking ownership of the process and maintaining control.

In other words, writers, release your inner badass.

Take charge. Think and act like a business investor, an entrepreneur, the publisher, the boss. You don't need to be a bully to be successful, but you need to be able to make decisions and communicate those decisions.

Maintain control. Delegate, but do not abdicate. No one cares about your book as much as you do. If you hand off your manuscript to a self-publishing service company, they won't put time and attention into it the way you would. They are motivated to sell you expensive services, not to create a book that sells. That's your job.

Don't sign anything you don't understand. In particular, read and understand everything regarding the granting of rights, licenses, and ownership. And make sure any contract may be terminated by you at any time. There are sharks out there.

Remember, everything is negotiable (almost). In our culture, we don't learn to haggle and negotiate on a day-to-day basis. It's considered impolite. We fear people will think less of us. The reality is, when it comes to business transactions, people will respect you more if you negotiate. The key to negotiation is preparation. Know what you want. Know your choices. Know your walk-away point. Even if you can't negotiate a better deal, you always have the choice of saying no.

Wear a business hat. The business side of writing will not run itself. Treat your business as a business. Set aside a particular time each week or month to take care of bookkeeping, recordkeeping, and business planning. Put it on your calendar. The buck starts and stops with you.

Admit your mistakes. If you signed on with the wrong company or freelancer, admit it and find a way out, even if it costs money.

Think big and think long. The chances of earning enough to quit your day job by publishing one book are slim. If you approach your writing career with a long-term view, realizing you will learn and improve along the way, you are less likely to burn out before reaching your goals.

Bottom line: treat your writing venture as a legitimate and laudable endeavor, something you and everyone around you should take seriously and admire. And success will follow.

APPENDIX

UNDERSTANDING KEY CONTRACT TERMS

As a self-published author, you are going to be entering into a lot of contracts. For many authors, this is the most uncomfortable task. One writer told me contracts look like 5,000 words run through a blender.

I encourage you to print out the contracts and work through them with a highlighter or pen. If you take the time, you will begin to see patterns and understand the concepts. Below are some hints.

The key provisions to understand are (i) what rights you are granting, (ii) how much control you will have over the publication and sales processes, (iii) how and when you will get paid, (iv) what are your potential liabilities, and (v) how to get out of the contact.

KINDLE DIRECT PUBLISHING TERMS AND CONDITIONS

Contract language	My interpretation
5.5 Grant of Rights. *You grant to each Amazon party,*	*Amazon party* means Amazon and all their affiliated companies worldwide.
throughout the term of this Agreement	In a later section, the Agreement says that either you or KDP may terminate at any time, so these words are acceptable.
a nonexclusive,	Always look for the word *nonexclusive*. You should not be granting anyone exclusive rights without understanding exactly what you are granting.
irrevocable	Not exactly. You may terminate KDP's right to sell your ebook, but they may continue to store a digital file and support ebooks already sold.
right and license to distribute Digital Books,	This is what you want to see—a nonexclusive right for a limited purpose, in this case distributing Digital Books.

Contract language	My interpretation
directly and through third-party distributors, in all digital formats by all digital distribution means available.	This phrase makes me uncomfortable. Is Amazon going to expand into digital formats other than Kindle and become an aggregator like Smashwords? I would not be surprised.
This right includes, without limitation, the right to: *reproduce, index and store Digital Books on one or more computer facilities, and reformat, convert and encode Digital Books;*	These are the rights they need to distribute your ebook. They make sense.
display, market, transmit, distribute, sell and otherwise digitally make available all or any portion of Digital Books through Amazon Properties for customers and prospective customers to download, access, copy and paste, print, annotate and/or view online and offline, including on portable devices;	*Amazon Properties* refers to their websites in various countries and any other Amazon app or sales channel. Most of this is fine, but I don't like the copy and paste part.
permit customers to "store" Digital Books that they have purchased from us on servers ("Virtual Storage") and to access and re-download such Digital Books from Virtual Storage from time to time both during and after the term of this Agreement;	This enables readers to move between devices and access their books from the "cloud." Sounds fine to me.

Contract language	*My interpretation*
(d) display and distribute *(i) your trademarks and logos in the form you provide them to us or within Digital Books (with such modifications as are necessary to optimize their viewing), and* *(ii) portions of Digital Books, in each case solely for the purposes of marketing, soliciting and selling Digital Books*	Good. The license to use any trademark or excerpt is appropriately limited.
and related Amazon offerings;	I do not know what they mean by *related Amazon offerings*. Perhaps it means related books and services. Typical Amazon—leaving doors open to new opportunities. The word *related* works in your favor. The door is not opened too wide.
(e) use, reproduce, adapt, modify, and distribute, as we determine appropriate, in our sole discretion, any metadata that you provide in connection with Digital Books; and	Metadata typically means your name, publication date, and other product information. I wonder what they plan to do with my metadata.
(f) transmit, reproduce and otherwise use (or cause the reformatting, transmission, reproduction, and/or other use of) Digital Books as mere technological incidents to and for the limited purpose of technically enabling the foregoing (e.g., caching to enable display).	Technical mumbo-jumbo.

Contract language	*My interpretation*
In addition, you agree that we may permit our affiliates and independent contractors, and our affiliates' independent contractors, to exercise the rights that you grant to us in this Agreement.	While I would prefer to have more control over who else may distribute my ebook, Amazon may permit others to do only what Amazon is permitted to do.
You grant us the rights set forth in this Section 5.5 on a worldwide basis; however, if we make available to you a procedure for indicating that you do not have worldwide distribution rights to a Digital Book, then the territory for the sale of that Digital Book will be those territories for which you indicate, through the procedure we provide to you, that you have distribution rights.	If you do not have worldwide rights to your ebook, you may limit the markets.
3. Term and Termination *We are entitled to terminate this Agreement and your access to your Program account at any time. We will notify you upon termination.*	In other provisions, they list reasons why they may terminate, such as your work infringes on someone else's copyright. This right to terminate for no reason is typical, so they do not have to justify their termination. It is an acceptable provision.
You are entitled to terminate at any time by providing us notice of termination, in which event we will cease selling your Digital Books within 5 business days from the date you provide us notice of termination.	This is what you want. The right to terminate at any time without payment of any termination fees.
Following termination, we may fulfill any customer orders for your Digital Books pending as of the date of termination or suspension,	Sounds reasonable.

Contract language	*My interpretation*
and we may continue to maintain digital copies of your Digital Books in order to provide continuing access to or re-downloads of your Digital Books or otherwise support customers who have purchased a Digital Book prior to termination or suspension. All rights to Digital Books acquired by customers will survive termination.	All this is reasonable. Anyone who has already purchased your ebook may download it again.
5.3.1 Providing Your List Price. *You will provide a list price through the KDP website for each Digital Book you submit to us.... You may change your List Price through the KDP website, and your change will be effective within 5 business days.*	Good. You want to control list price.
5.3.4 Customer Prices. *To the extent not prohibited by applicable laws, we have sole and complete discretion to set the retail customer price at which your Digital Books are sold through the Program.*	Amazon may discount the price of your ebook. However, later in the contract they explain that royalty payments are based upon the list price you choose, so their discounting your ebook will not discount your royalties.
We are solely responsible for processing payments, payment collection, requests for refunds and related customer service, and will have sole ownership and control of all data obtained from customers and prospective customers in connection with the Program.	They will not tell you who bought your ebook. This is typical of Amazon—holding onto information.

Contract language	My interpretation
5.4.2 When We Pay You. *Each Amazon party will pay Royalties due on Digital Book sales approximately 60 days following the end of the calendar month during which the sales were made. At the time of payment, we will make available to you an online report detailing sales of Digital Books and corresponding Royalties.*	Nice and clear.
5.4.6 Payment Disputes. *You may not bring a suit or other legal proceeding against us with regard to any statement unless you bring it within six months after the date the statement is available.*	Frankly, I don't know how you could contest a payment since you have no access to the underlying sales information. This is a problem even in traditional publishing.
5.8 Representations, Warranties and Indemnities. *You represent and warrant that:* *(a) you have the full right, power and authority to enter into and fully perform this Agreement and will comply with the terms of this Agreement;*	Among other things, this means that you are at least 18 years old and have the mental capacity to enter into a contract, and that you have whatever authority you need from others to grant the licenses and enter into this contract.
(b) prior to you or your designee's delivery of any content, you will have obtained all rights that are necessary for the exercise of the rights granted under this Agreement;	You are assuring them that you have the right to sell your ebook, because you either own the copyright or have obtained all the necessary permissions, licenses, and rights.

Contract language	My interpretation
(c) neither the exercise of the rights authorized under this Agreement nor any materials embodied in the content nor its sale or distribution as authorized in this Agreement will violate or infringe upon the intellectual property, proprietary or other rights of any person or entity, including, without limitation, contractual rights, copyrights, trademarks, common law rights, rights of publicity, or privacy, or moral rights, or contain defamatory material or violate any laws or regulations of any jurisdiction;	You are responsible if your work is infringing, defamatory, or illegal, so make sure it isn't!
(d) you will ensure that all Digital Books delivered under the Program comply with the technical delivery specifications provided by us; and	Technical requirements are on their website.
(e) you will be solely responsible for accounting and paying any co-owners or co-administrators of any Digital Book or portion thereof any royalties with respect to the uses of the content and their respective shares, if any, of any monies payable under this Agreement.	Amazon won't split the payments among co-writers. They will deliver payments to a single account. It's up to you to arrange for sharing royalties with any co-writers.

Contract language	*My interpretation*
To the fullest extent permitted by applicable law, you will indemnify, defend and hold Amazon, its officers, directors, employees, affiliates, subcontractors and assigns harmless from and against any loss, claim, liability, damage, action or cause of action (including reasonable attorneys' fees) that arises from any breach of your representations, warranties or obligations set forth in this Agreement.	This means that if Amazon or anyone else on the list is sued because any of the statements in (a) through (e) are incorrect, or you otherwise breach the contract, you will be obligated to pay the attorneys and all costs and damages for everyone on their list.
We will be entitled, at our expense, to participate in the defense and settlement of the claim or action with counsel of our own choosing.	They will hire their own attorneys, and you will pay their attorneys if you breach the contract.

CREATESPACE SERVICES AGREEMENT

I have deleted the terms that apply to MP3s and videos.

Contract language	My interpretation
6. Licenses; Ownership; Feedback. **6.1 Content** *Subject to your retained control and ownership of your Content as described in Section 6.4. [I think they mean 6.2, which is below] in order to enable us to provide you with the Services on your behalf, you grant to us a nonexclusive license,*	Good. You want the license to be nonexclusive, so you can use other POD providers as well.
during the term of this Agreement, to…	In another section, it says either party may terminate at any time.
(c) with respect to Books, print, distribute and sell your Book through the CreateSpace E-stores, the Amazon Properties and other sales channels,…	This is what you want to see—a non-exclusive license for a limited purpose—printing and selling your books. Nothing more.

Contract language	My interpretation
You grant us the rights set forth in this Section 6.1 on a worldwide basis; however, if we make available to you a procedure for indicating that you do not have worldwide distribution rights to a Title, then the territory for the sale of that Title will be those territories for which you indicate, through the procedure we provide to you, that you have distribution rights.	Similar to KDP contract.
6.2 Ownership *Subject to the licenses set forth in this Section 6,... as between the parties, you retain all right, title and interest in and to the Content, including all patent, copyright, trademark, service mark, mask work, moral right, trade secret or other intellectual property or proprietary right (collectively, "Intellectual Property Rights") therein.*	This is what you want to see. Other than the specific licenses granted, you retain all other rights and ownership in your work.

Contract language	My interpretation
10. Term; Termination *This Agreement will remain in effect until terminated in accordance with this Section. You may terminate this Agreement at any time by giving notice to us, and we may terminate this Agreement at any time by sending you an e-mail notice at the e-mail address associated with your account. Our notice of such termination will be effective at the time we send you the notice.*	Good. You want to be able to terminate at any time.
Upon termination, you will pay us whatever fees were incurred prior to the date of the termination.	CreateSpace provides a number of publishing services. Most likely you will have paid the fees in advance. Some fees are refundable if you are not satisfied. Check their website.
Also upon termination: *(a) we may fulfill any Customer orders pending as of the date of termination... .*	This is reasonable.

Contract language	My interpretation
Upon termination, we may set off against any payments to be made to you, an amount determined by us to be adequate to cover any disputes, chargebacks and refunds from your account for a prospective three-month period. At the end of such three-month period following termination, we will refund any amount not used to offset chargebacks and refunds to you, or seek reimbursement from you via any of the means authorized in Section 5.1 above for any additional amount required to offset chargebacks and refunds, as applicable.	This gives them the right to hold back any payments to you to cover returns or claims. A three-month holdback period is reasonable.
5.1 Fees *For any Unit sold to a Customer, we will pay you the applicable Content License Royalty based on the List Price of the Unit:* *(a) within 31 days after the end of the month in which the Unit sold for physical Units sold through the CreateSpace E-Stores and the Amazon Properties; and (b) within 60 days after the end of the month in which the Unit is sold for physical Units sold through Expanded Distribution.*	Timing of payments is clear and reasonable. As with the KDP contract, you set the list price, but CreateSpace/Amazon may discount the retail price. Royalties, however, are based upon the list price you choose. I do not have a problem with that.

Contract language	My interpretation
7. Representations and Warranties *You acknowledge that we are not the publisher of your Titles (including your Content). You represent and warrant that you will be the publisher of your Titles (including your Content) and, in any case, that you will bear the full and ultimate responsibility for the publication and general distribution of your Titles (including your Content).*	By stating that you are the "publisher," CreateSpace is saying you are responsible for the contents of your work; they are merely a printer or "conduit." Being the "publisher" is a shorthand phrase for a bundle of rights and responsibilities. This is acceptable.
You further represent and warrant that you will comply with all laws, rules, regulations and orders of any governmental authority having jurisdiction over your performance hereunder as applicable in each country (including any local legal requirements with respect to your publication of your Titles, such as making any necessary notifications and filings of copies of your Titles	Consider this a "risk-allocation" provision. Since you cannot say that you *know* your content complies with the laws of every jurisdiction worldwide (there is no way to know that without hiring a team of international lawyers), then you are saying that if it turns out that filings or other steps must be taken in other jurisdictions and countries, you are the one responsible for those filings and actions. This is a risk you are taking and is reasonable.

Contract language	**My interpretation**
(b) you have all requisite right, power and authority to enter into this Agreement and perform your obligations hereunder;	This means you are at least 18 years old and have the mental capacity to enter into a contract, and that you have whatever authority you need from others to grant the licenses and enter into this contract with CreateSpace. It is reasonable.
(c) prior to your delivery of Content to us you have or have obtained all rights, clearances and permissions to grant the licenses you grant hereunder that are necessary for us to exercise the rights you grant under this Agreement without any further payment obligation by us,...	You are warranting that you have the right to publish your ebook, either because you own the copyright or have obtained all the necessary permissions, licenses, and rights.
(d) you are granting us the rights, licenses and authorizations you grant hereunder free and clear of any encumbrances, and this Agreement does not violate or conflict with any other arrangements, understandings or agreements between you and any third party;	Encumbrances means liens or other restrictions. Here you are warranting that you will not be violating any other contract by publishing through CreateSpace. For instance, you have not granted to anyone else the exclusive right to publish your book, you are not violating any non-competition or right of first offer in a traditional publishing contract, and you are not violating any agreement with your co-authors.

Contract language	My interpretation
(e) the Content (and our use thereof) is not defamatory, libelous, obscene, or otherwise illegal, does not invade any right of privacy, and does not infringe upon any Intellectual Property Right or right of publicity of any person or entity, and any recipe, formula, or instruction contained in the Content is accurate and is not injurious to the user;	Once again, a risk-allocation provision. If your book is defamatory or otherwise harmful, you are responsible, not CreateSpace or Amazon.
(f) the Content complies with all aspects of the Content Guidelines as such may be updated from time to time; and	The phrase *Content Guidelines* is a link to the page listing these guidelines. This is an example of "incorporation by reference," which means those provisions are made a part of this Agreement. Most online agreements contain multiple links. You should click through to read them.
(g) you are and will be solely responsible for accounting and paying any co-owners or co-administrators of any Content any royalties with respect to the uses of the Content permitted hereunder and their respective shares, if any, of any monies payable hereunder.	You, not CreateSpace, are responsible for paying any co-authors.

Contract language	My interpretation
8.1 Indemnification *You will indemnify, defend and hold us and our affiliates (and the respective employees, directors, members, managers and representatives of each) and any operator of an Amazon Property harmless from and against any and all claims, judgments, damages and expenses (including without limitation reasonable attorneys' fees) (collectively, "Claims")*	This means that if Amazon or anyone else on the list is sued because any of your representations or warranties are incorrect or because you breach the contract in any manner, you will be required to pay all attorneys' costs and damages.
arising out of any breach or alleged breach by you of the terms of this Agreement, including without limitation the terms contained within the Products and Help pages and the Content Guidelines and Privacy Notice, which are incorporated herein by reference.	Again, the capitalized words are links, another example of incorporating other provisions into this contract. The Help pages alone are endless. This process makes the contract harder to read.

Both the KDP and CreateSpace contracts say that Amazon may change the terms and conditions at any time by posting the changes online, and that your continued use of their services is your agreement to those changes. I do not like these provisions. I used to hope that the courts would find them unenforceable, but many courts have upheld them, at least when it comes to the payment of fees. If Amazon tries to expand the scope of its license without providing writers additional notice, I hope courts will not enforce that unilateral expansion.

You will find similar provisions in the terms and conditions of other POD providers and social media sites. You may have no choice but to agree and take your chances.

AN EGREGIOUS CONTRACT

BEFORE YOU JUDGE Amazon too harshly, take a look at the following provisions from one SPSC contract. I will not disclose the name because I fear they will come after me. But as of late 2013, the following zingers were in their Terms and Conditions.

Contract language	*My interpretation*
2. Granting of Rights *The Author transfers to the Publisher without limitation of place the* **exclusive right of reproduction and dissemination** *(Publisher's right) of the work* **for the duration of statutory copyright** *including all additional bibliographical texts and/or images supplied by the Author (e.g., cover text, biographical details) for all print and electronic editions (e-book) and for all print runs without limit of units and in all language versions. In the case of works which have already been published by other publishing houses, a non-exclusive right of use shall be transferred. The*	If you sign on to this agreement, you are granting the publisher *exclusive* right to publish your book (and all accompanying images and text) in print and electronic formats for the life of the copyright (your life plus 70 years). This is shocking. Don't be fooled by the last sentence, which states that the author continues to be the copyright holder. If you have granted them exclusive right of reproduction and dissemination, then you cannot publish your book elsewhere.
Author shall continue to be the copyright holder of his work.	

Contract language	My interpretation
3. Duties and Rights of the Publisher *Design, layout guidelines and delivery dates shall be determined by the Publisher. Sales prices, publishing brand and marketing shall also be determined by the Publisher.*	Remember the concept of controlling your work. You would have no control under this contract.
4. Royalty *For each copy (print or e-book) sold and paid for, Author shall receive a royalty of 12% of the average remuneration received by Publisher…Royalties shall be settled every twelve months for the preceding year.*	This low royalty rate is more in line with traditional publishing contracts under which you would have received an advance. They pay only once a year.
The contractual parties agree that royalty claims of the Author shall only be disbursed if monthly average royalty claims…exceed 50 Euros (about $68) per month…Author shall, instead of a royalty payment, receive a book voucher to the same value which he may freely redeem for all titles produced by the Publisher.	So if your average monthly royalties (not sales) are less than $68 a month ($816 per year), you get a book voucher and no money. Can it get any worse than this?

BOTTOM LINE

Read and understand your contracts before signing, particularly everything regarding the grant of rights.

RESOURCES

Books

Bielstein, Susan M. *Permissions, A Survival Guide.* Chicago: The University of Chicago Press, 2006.

Bunnin, Brad and Beren, Peter. *The Writers Legal Companion.* New York: Basic Books, 1998.

Butler, Joy R. *The Permission Seeker's Guide Through the Legal Jungle.* Arlington, VA: Sashay Communications, LLC, 2007.

Carter, Ruth. *The Legal Side of Blogging: How Not To Get Sued, Fired, Arrested or Killed.* Jents, LLC, 2013.

Crawford, Ted. *Business and Legal Forms for Authors and Self-Publishers.* New York: Allworth Press, 1999.

Duboff, Leonard D. and Krages, Bert P. *Law (In Plain English) for Writers.* Naperville, IL: Sphinx Publishing, 2005.

Fishman, Stephen. *The Public Domain.* Berkeley, CA; NOLO Press, 2014.

Friedlander, Joel and Sargent, Betty Kelly. *The Self-Publisher's Ultimate Resource Guide.* San Rafael, CA; Marin Bookworks, 2016.

Kawasaki, Guy and Welch, Shawn. *APE; Author, Publisher, Entrepreneur; How To Publish A Book.* Nononina Press, 2013.

Lee, Bonnie, E.A. *Taxpertise: The Complete Book of Dirty Little Secrets.* Irvine, CA: Entrepreneur Press, 2009.

Levine, Mark. *The Fine Print of Self-Publishing, Sixth Edition.* Minneapolis, MN: Bascom Publishing Group, 2016.

McHale, Robert, Esq. with Gurulay, Eric. *Navigating Social Media Legal Risk: Safeguarding Your Business.* Indianapolis, IN: QUE Publishing, 2012.

Murray, Kay and Crawford, Tad. *The Writer's Legal Guide; Fourth Edition.* New York: Allworth Press, 2013.

Randolph, Sallie; Davis, Stacy; Elia, Anthony; and Dustman, Karen. *Author Law A to Z.* Sterling, VA: Capital Books, Inc., 2005.

Rich, Jason R. *Self-Publishing For Dummies.* Hoboken, NJ: Wiley Publishing, Inc., 2006.

Ross, Orna and Sedwick, Helen. *How Authors Sell Publishing Rights*, Font Publications, 2016.

Stim, Richard. Getting Permission. Berkeley, CA; NOLO Press, 2013.

Websites

(Also on my website: http://helensedwick.com/resources/)

- IRS site for obtaining a Federal Employer Identification Number (EIN): http://www.irs.gov/Businesses/Small-Businesses-&-Self-Employed/ Apply-for-an-Employer-Identification-Number-%28EIN%29-Online

- Library of Congress Control Number: (http://www.loc.gov/publish/pcn/)

- U.S. Patent and Trademark Office trademark searches: https://www.uspto.gov/trademarks-application-process/search-trademark-database

- R.R. Bowker for buying ISBNs: https://www.myidentifiers.com/get-your-isbn-now

- Bay Area Editors Forum list of editing options: http://www.editorsforum.org/what_do_ sub_pages/definitions_copyediting.php

- U.S. Copyright Office Information Circulars: http://www.copyright.gov/circs/

- Searching for copyright owners: http://www.copyright.gov/records/

- For international searches, The University of Cambridge: http://www.caret.cam.ac.uk/copyright/Page48.html
- Copyright expiration chart from Cornell University: http://copyright.cornell.edu/resources/publicdomain.cfm
- Stanford University Fair Use project: http://cyberlaw.stanford.edu/focus-areas/copyright-and-fair-use.

To identify the owner of an ISP:

- http://www.whois.net/
- http://www.domaintools.com/research/dns/

Sample takedown notices:

- The National Press Photographers Association site: https://nppa.org/page/5617
- IP Watchdog also provides a sample: http://www.ipwatchdog.com/2009/07/06/sample-dmca-take-down-letter/
- The Electronic Frontier Foundation (EFF) and the Takedown Hall of Shame: https://www.eff.org/takedowns

Sites for researching the reputation of SPSCs, POD, agents and publishers:

- Absolute Write Water Cooler: http://www.absolutewrite.com/forums/
- Independent Publisher's Magazine: http://www.independentpublisher.com/
- Independent Publishing Magazine: http://www.theindependentpublishingmagazine.com/
- Predators and Editors: http://pred-ed.com/
- Writer Beware: http://accrispin.blogspot.co.uk/

There are thousands of websites and blogs offering useful advice to writers and self-publishers. In fact, if you search the web, you are risking information overload. Below if a list of my favorite self-publishing blogs and websites, in no particular order. There are countless others.

- Joel Friedlander's The Book Designer: http://www.thebookdesigner.com/

- Jane Friedman: http://janefriedman.com/

- Joanna Penn: http://www.thecreativepenn.com/

- Nina Amir: http://ninaamir.com/

- Alliance of Independent Authors: https://www.allianceindependentauthors.org/

- Author U: http://authoru.org/

- Frances Caballo: http://socialmediajustforwriters.com/

- Arlene Miller, The Grammar Diva: http://bigwords101.com/

- Aaron Shepard Publishing Blog: http://www.newselfpublishing.com/blog/

ABOUT THE AUTHOR

Helen Sedwick is a California attorney with thirty years of experience representing businesses and entrepreneurs as diverse as wineries, graphic designers, green toy makers, software engineers, restaurateurs, and writers. Her historical nove, Coyote Winds has earned five-star reviews from ForeWord Reviews and is an IndieBRAG Medallion Honoree.

Helen is a member of the Board of Advisors of the Alliance of Independent Authors and a Contributing Writer for TheBookDesigner.com and BookWorks. Helen's blog coaches writers on everything from saving on taxes to avoiding scams.

As a small-business owner and published author, she understand the challenges of balancing legal, business, and creative concerns. She wrote the *Self-Publisher's Legal Handbook* to help writers publish and promote their work while minimizing the legal risks.

ACKNOWLEDGMENTS

I could not have finished this book without the help of talented and dedicated professionals. I want to thank Mark Chimsky for his editorial skills and his insights about the publishing world; Arlene Miller (the Grammar Diva) for her attention to detail and style; Patricia Zylius copyeditor extraordinaire; Damonza.com for their clean and polished cover and layout design; Frances Caballo for demystifying social media; Kate McMillan for creating the website of my dreams; Joyce Smail for tax guidance; my friends at Redwood Writers for urging me to tackle this project; and Howard Klepper for his endless patience, support, and humor.

INDEX

R

Resale Certificate: 82, 87, 90, 102, 110
Right of Publicity: 38, 41, 44

S

Sales and Use Tax: 82, 88, 108
Self-Employment Tax: 106, 107
Seller's Permit: 82
SLAPP: 50
Stock Image: 28, 88

T

Takedown notice: 14, 89, 169
Titles: 12
Trademark: 33, 34, 54, 79
Translations: 138

W

W-9: 74, 105, 107, 111

Made in the USA
Las Vegas, NV
11 February 2021